U0727267

我们的生活在于行动，而不是时间；在于思想，而不是呼吸；在于感觉，而不是表盘上的数字。我们应该按心灵的悸动来计算时间。谁思考最多，情操最高尚，做得最好，谁的生活就最有意义。

We live in deeds, not years; in thoughts, not breaths; in feelings, not in figures on a dial. We should count time by heart-throbs. He most lives who thinks most, feels the noblest, acts the best.

致十年后的自己

何之遥/编译

江苏人民出版社

图书在版编目（CIP）数据

致十年后的自己：英汉对照 / 何之遥编译．-- 南京：江苏人民出版社，2016.1
ISBN 978-7-214-12858-4

Ⅰ．①致… Ⅱ．①何… Ⅲ．①英语－汉语－对照读物 Ⅳ．① H319.4

中国版本图书馆 CIP 数据核字（2015）第 315145 号

书　　名	致十年后的自己：英汉对照
编 译 者	何之遥
责任编辑	朱　超
装帧设计	浪殿设计　飞　扬
版式设计	张文艺
出版发行	凤凰出版传媒股份有限公司 江苏人民出版社
出版社地址	南京市湖南路1号A楼，邮编：210009
出版社网址	http://www.jspph.com http://jsrmcbs.tmall.com
经　　销	凤凰出版传媒股份有限公司
印　　刷	北京中印联印务有限公司
开　　本	718 毫米 ×1000 毫米 1/16
印　　张	12
字　　数	141 千字
版　　次	2016 年 5 月第 1 版　2016 年 5 月第 1 次印刷
标准书号	978-7-214-12858-4
定　　价	24.00元

A Letter to Myself in Ten Years

致十年后的自己

前 言 | PREFACE

Years Gone By
逝水流年

◎ A. Potter

As one year goes by and

another one begins.

It makes us remember

things that have happened and the has-beens.

Remember that and remember this,

what about the times, and why did that happens.

When did childhood end and adulthood start?

As you look back on the stages of life,

remember everything you can.

From mistakes, to accomplishments, to lessons learned.

Because we know that nothing's without strife.

But in the end, no matter what else will be.

You will always have friends and family.

Remember the ones who were there during the "ifs", "buts", "whens", or "whys".

The ones who've been there during the years gone by.

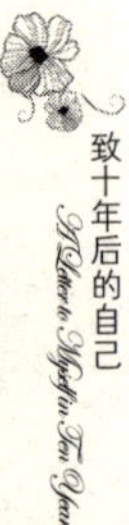

一年过去

又一年开始

我们总会想起

往日的种种

历历在目

逝去的时光，不堪回首的往事

遥远的童年，苦涩的青春

回首过去

拾起记忆的碎片

错误，成功，教训

纷纷扰扰

最终，无论如何

你总还有家人、朋友

在人生的跌宕起伏中

陪伴你走过一年又一年

目 录 | CONTENTS

在追忆中成长

勇于活在当下

CONTENTS 目录

永不放弃梦

写给未来的自己

在追忆中成长

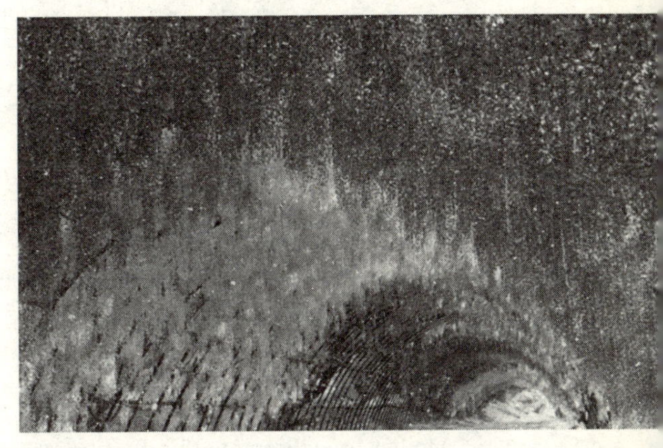

The best and most beautiful things in the world cannot be seen nor even touched, but just felt in the heart.

——Helen Keller

世界上最好和最美丽的事物，用眼睛看不见，用手摸不到，只能用心去体会。

——海伦·凯勒

A Time for Memoriese

松树下的生命轮回

◎ Sharon Wright

One **balmy**[1] summer afternoon, I sat on an old blanket under a pine tree chatting with my mother. For years, we had been coming to this park for family picnics and gatherings, and my mother and I often sat in this same spot.

In recent years, we usually just talked about life, but sometimes we recalled events from my childhood. Like the time I was thirteen and had my first date, when Mother brought me to this spot under the tree and told me about the facts of life. Or the time a few years later, when my hair turned out pink for my senior prom and she'd held me while I cried. But the most special event that occurred next to this tree was when I told Mother I was getting married. Tears filled her eyes and this time I held her while she cried. She told me she was sad to lose her little girl but happy to see that I had turned into a beautiful young woman.

Over the years, we'd watched the pine trees in this park grow tall and straight until their needles seemed to touch the clouds. Each year of their growth seemed to match our increasingly close relationship and the deepening love we had for each other.

On this particular sunny afternoon, Mother and I sat quietly breathing in the

① balmy ['bɑ:mi] a. 芳香的，温和的

美丽语录

The memory of my mother and her teachings were, after all, the only capital I had to start life with, and on that capital I have made my way.

—Andrew Jackson

对母亲的记忆和母亲的教诲是我人生起步的唯一资本，它奠定了我的人生之路。

——安德鲁·杰克逊

一个阳光和煦的夏日午后，公园大松树下的地上铺了一层老旧的地毯，我和母亲坐在上面静静地聊天。多年以来，我们一直在这个公园举行家庭聚会、野餐，而我和母亲就时常坐在这棵松树下。

最近这些年，我们大多数只是谈论生活，但有时也会回忆我童年时代的一些往事。比如，13 岁那年我第一次约会，母亲就把我带到这里，在松树下告诉了我很多生活的真谛；比如，又过了几年，即将从中学毕业的我，变成了一个染着粉红色头发的叛逆少女，而就在这棵松树下，我紧紧地依偎在母亲怀里失声痛哭。但是，最让人难忘的是，在这棵松树下，我告诉母亲我要结婚了。那一刻，喜悦的泪水溢满了她的眼眶，我紧紧地搂住母亲。她说，此刻，她既为即将失去她的小女孩而难过，也为她的小女孩终于长成美丽的年轻女子而欣喜不已。

多年来，我们眼看着这棵松树越长越高，越来越直，逐渐长成直逼云霄的参天大树。它的成长恰似母亲与我的关系；随着岁月的流逝，我们越来越亲密，对彼此的爱也越来越深。

在这个阳光灿烂的午后，草坪刚刚修过，我和母亲静静地坐着，呼吸

scent of freshly mown grass. She was unusually solemn and took me by surprise when she asked me, "Who will you bring here after I'm gone?"

I gave her one of my arched-eyebrow inquiries, then smiled. After a few moments, when she didn't return my smile, I began to wonder what made her ask such a **disturbing**[①] question. Mother picked up a blade of grass and began to shred it with her fingernail. I'd become well acquainted with my mother's habits, and this particular one indicated she had something serious on her mind.

For several minutes, we sat in silence gathering our thoughts. A couple of blue jays **squawked**[②] nearby and an airplane flew overhead, but they didn't ease the awkward moment between us. Finally, I reached over and took my mother's hand in mine. "There's nothing you can't tell me, Mother," I said. "We will handle this together, like we always have."

She looked into my face, and her eyes filled with tears that spilt down her cheeks that were **alarmingly**[③] pale. Even before she said it, I knew what was coming. Mother was dying.

I held her tightly while she told me that her heart condition was worsening and couldn't be repaired. I think I had known for quite a while but had not been willing to admit it to myself. She'd had several heart attacks and, a few years ago, even open-heart surgery. What I didn't know, and what she had kept from me, was that her condition wasn't improving. We talked about her options, which were few; we cried, held each other and wished for more time together.

That was many years ago now. Mother died soon after that day, before my sons had a chance to know her. I still come to the park, but now I bring my boys.

---

① disturbing [di'stə:biŋ] a. 烦扰的，担心的，令人不安的

② squawk [skwɔ:k] v. 呱呱地叫鸣，喋喋不休地发牢骚

③ alarmingly [ə'lɑ:miŋli] ad. 让人担忧地

着空气中弥漫着的青草芳香。她显得格外沉默而肃穆。出乎意料地，她忽然问我道："在我走了以后，你会带谁来这里呢？"

我不禁扬起了眉毛，惊讶地想要问点什么，却又很快露出了一丝微笑。过了很久，她仍旧对我的微笑没有丝毫回应。我开始疑惑她为什么会问这样一个让人不安的问题。母亲捡起一片青草，用指甲不停地撕扯着。我对母亲的习惯非常熟悉，这个动作意味着她的脑海里正在思考很重要的事情。

有那么一会儿，我们安静地坐着，只是整理着自己的思绪。一对蓝色松鸦在不远处嘎嘎地惊叫着，飞机从我们头顶上一掠而过，但这一切似乎都没能缓和我们之间的尴尬气氛。后来，我伸出双手，紧紧握住母亲的手，说道："妈妈，这世上没有什么事是你不能和我说的。让我们一起来面对吧，就像我们一直以来的那样。"

她看着我，脸色苍白得惊人。她的眼泪夺眶而出，洒落在她的双颊上。在她开口说话之前，我已然明白：母亲已经老了，来日无多了。

我将她紧紧地抱在怀中。她告诉我说，她的心脏功能正在不断恶化，很可能无法康复。其实，相当长的一段时间以来，我就知道她的病情不容乐观，只不过心里一直不愿意承认这个事实罢了。几年前，她多次突发心脏病，甚至接受了心脏手术。但我不知道的是，她一直对我隐瞒了真实病情，谎称她的情况在不断地好转。我们谈到了她面前极其有限的几种选择，忍不住抱头痛哭起来，但愿我们在一起的时间能再多一点，再长一点。

那天之后不久，母亲就去世了，甚至还来不及看一眼她即将出生的外孙们。转眼间，很多年过去了。我依然时不时地会去公园，只不过现在是

I still sit under that same sturdy pine tree on an old blanket and talk to my sons of family picnics, gatherings and the grandmother they never knew. Just as my mother did with me, I tell my children about their youthful antics and praise them for their accomplishments as young adults. We come to this special place to create our own memories that I know would make my mother smile with pride.

Not long ago my oldest son wanted to come to the park and talk, so we came and sat under our tree. He hemmed and hawed for a few minutes, then he finally told me he was getting married. I cried tears of joy as my son hugged me—his hug a rare and special treat. I told him how proud I was of the man he had become.

As I sat there that cool April afternoon soaking up the sun and the smell of freshly mown grass, I felt I had come full circle under this giant pine tree. Holding my son in my arms, I was happy for him, just the way I knew my mother had been happy for me all those years ago when I told her I was getting married.

Looking over my son's shoulder, I saw that several young pine saplings had been planted recently. As these trees grow straight and tall, I thought, will the lives of my family continue to grow with them? I wanted to share this spot with my grandchildren, too.

The branches above were swaying in the breeze and in them I heard a whispering voice: Who will you bring here when I'm gone? It was my mother's voice, and I tightened my arms around my son.

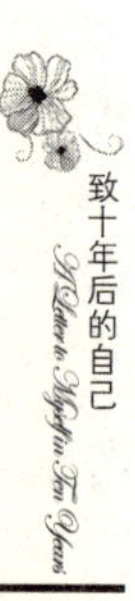

带着我的儿子们一起。我还会坐在那棵粗壮的大松树下，坐在那老旧的地毯上，向儿子们回忆起在这里办过的家庭聚会和野餐，还有他们未曾谋面的外祖母。我也会像母亲对我一样，对儿子们诉说他们年幼时的种种趣事，赞扬他们成年后取得的种种成绩。我们来到这个拥有特殊意义的地方，创造属于我们自己的回忆，而这些甜蜜的回忆，我相信，一定会让在天有灵的母亲倍感欣慰与骄傲。

不久前，我的大儿子想来公园与我谈谈。于是，我们来到了那棵大松树下坐了下来。一开始他支支吾吾，闪烁其词，后来终于鼓起勇气告诉我说，他要结婚了。一时之间，我喜极而泣，而他紧紧地拥抱着我。要知道，这对他来说是多么罕见而特殊的举动。我对他说，你终于长大了，成为男子汉了，我为你感到骄傲。

凉爽四月的下午，我坐在那里，沐浴着春日的阳光，嗅着草坪的清香，忽然发觉我的人生在这棵大松树下完成了圆满的轮回。我用双臂拥抱着儿子，为他感到高兴，就如同许多年以前，母亲在听闻我即将嫁为人妇时为我感到高兴一样。

从儿子的肩上望过去，我看到几株新栽的松树苗，心想：当这些树苗长得笔直挺拔、高耸入云时，我的家人也会伴随着它们一起成长吗？我也想和孙子孙女们分享这里的一切。

树枝在微风中婆娑摇曳着，仿佛有阵阵窃窃私语在耳畔浮现：在我走了以后，你会带谁来这里呢？不错，那是我母亲的声音。我不禁将儿子抱得更紧了。

The Mother Box
母亲之盒

© Linda Webb Gustafson

Late one December evening, bathed in the soft light of the Christmas tree, I lay on the couch with my eyes closed, letting my memories **swirl**[①] around in pools of thought. Returning to the present, I opened my eyes and immediately my gaze fell upon a beautiful miniature Christmas city that lined my fireplace mantel. Well, it was really only half a city, as my dad had divided it between my sister and me twenty-five years earlier after our mother had passed away.

Little twinkle lights glowed from behind red cellophane windows in the tiny cardboard houses that had lined the living-room bookshelves of my childhood.

With no warning, the words tumbled out like a spilled glass of aged wine words that had been hidden in my heart a long time, waiting to surface, "Mom, I miss you so much."

An ocean of tears **ebbed**[②] and flowed for nearly an hour, and then the idea emerged. If I felt this way then surely my brother and sister did, too. Twenty-five years, five senses, one box that's what I would do I would capture the essence of my mother and place her in a box a Mother Box one for each of her children.

---

① swirl [swə:l] v.（使）成漩涡，盘旋，眩晕

② ebb [eb] v. 落潮，衰退

美丽语录

Youth fades; love droops; the leaves of friendship fall. A mother's secret hope outlives them all.

—Oliver Wendell Holmes

青春会逝去；爱情会枯萎；友谊的绿叶也会凋零。而一个母亲内心的希望比它们都要长久。

——奥利弗·温戴尔·荷马

12 月的一个深夜，屋内圣诞树的灯光柔和而又温馨，我闭着眼睛躺在沙发上，思绪游荡开去，回忆起种种往事来。当我张开双眼回到现实中时，我的目光忽然落在壁炉架上陈列着的精美的圣诞之城微缩模型上。事实上，那只不过是半个模型罢了。25 年前母亲去世时，父亲把这个微缩模型的一半分给了姐姐，另一半分给了我。

在我小的时候，这座小小的纸板房总是放在客厅的书架上。红色玻璃纸做的窗户，后面装着一闪一闪的小灯，宛如星星在眨着眼睛。

没有任何征兆地，长久以来深藏在我心底的一句话，突然就像一杯打翻的陈年红酒一般倾泄而出："妈妈，我是如此地想念你。"

在接下来的一小时里，我哭哭停停，不知流了多少眼泪，直到心里忽然间冒出一个主意来。我想，如果我对母亲的感觉如此强烈，那么我的兄弟姐妹们也一定感同身受。我要把这 25 年的时间通过五种感官做成一只盒子——一只"母亲之盒"，每只盒子里放入代表母亲特质的东西，分别送给兄弟姐妹们。

I began to think of our mother in terms of what scent encompassed her, what look best described her, what sound echoed "Mother", and so on.

Including my ten-year-old daughter, Shiloah, in my quest, we searched to put together pieces of a grandmother she'd never met.

First came the box all the memories would be housed in. Such a vast display we found. Flowered ones of every type ever found in a garden, ones with stars on them, moons, old-fashioned Victorian images, hearts and ones with Christmas themes, and then we saw them angels! Yes, for a mother no longer of this Earth, it was perfect. But, there were only two. One sister, one brother I'd make one for myself another time.

Oddly enough, the entire day was like that. We'd find two of just what we needed, no more, no less. With mounting excitement we took our treasures home and wrapped them with great love.

A river of memories wound its way through a thickly wooded forest of words, painting a picture of a thousand yesterdays, growing straight and tall like new seedlings among the old growth. Sealed with a simple envelope, they awaited their intended.

Just the right time presented itself to give my brother his box. As his eyes fell upon its contents, this man of thirty-seven was reduced to tears. My father was standing there, and I'll never forget the faraway look on his face. The years were melting away with each item my brother lifted from the Mother Box.

A package of grits representing a woman who grew up in the South and served it to her children for breakfast in Oregon, her favorite Johnny Mathis music, a shiny silver Christmas bow that felt like the party dresses she wore, a single silk red rose representing dozens my father had given her. I included the famous story of how once when they were courting, he brought long-stemmed

我开始回想，什么香味是母亲身上特有的，什么样子最能代表母亲，什么声音最能唤起对母亲的回忆，如此种种。

我们开始努力拼凑关于母亲的记忆碎片，就连我那 10 岁的女儿夏洛伊，也在我的要求下帮忙搜寻从未见过的外祖母的点点滴滴。

最重要的是，这个盒子必须包含我们对母亲的所有回忆。我们找到了很多很多，比如，花园里能找到的各种花朵，带有星星或月亮的各种物品，老式的维多利亚女王头像，心型纪念品以及各种圣诞饰物。我们还找到了天使图案的纪念品。的确，对于已然去世的母亲来说，天使是最完美的纪念物。但是，我们只找到了两个，一个给我姐姐，一个给我哥哥。我只能下次再给自己重新做一个了。

非常奇怪的是，一天下来，我们找到的每种纪念物都只有两个，不多不少。每当找到什么东西时，我们总是异常兴奋，满怀爱意，然后小心翼翼地将其包好，把我们的宝贝带回家去。

回忆就像一条蜿蜒曲折的河流，穿过茂密的丛林，绘出一幅由成千上万个昨日组成的美丽画卷。新的回忆，如同新长成的幼苗，在老树旁越长越高，越长越挺拔。回忆也像一封往日的信札，用朴素的信封简单封缄，在预定的时间被送至收信人手中，不早不晚，恰到好处。

我在适当的时候把盒子送给了我的哥哥。当他看见盒子里的物品时，这个 37 岁的男人忍不住潸然泪下。那时，我父亲也站在旁边，他脸上若有所思的表情让我永生难忘。看着我哥哥将盒中之物一件一件地取出，这么多年的岁月顷刻间都融化成浓浓的回忆。

一包粗燕麦粉，尽管我们住在俄勒冈州，但在南方长大的母亲经常喂孩子们吃这种食物；她最喜爱的约翰·马西斯的音乐唱片；一枚闪亮的银质蝴蝶结，看上去非常像她穿过的晚礼服的风格；一朵真丝红玫瑰，代表

roses that were as long as he was tall! She adored red roses. Finally, a bottle of her favorite perfume, Emeraude. I could hardly believe they still made it, but there it was, that familiar green. The shape of the bottle had changed over the years, but when I sprayed the misty fragrance into the air, it was unmistakably the scent of our mother.

This journey of the heart, traveled with my daughter, brought us together in spirit. We were both bound with the cords of love from the life of a woman long gone, yet still sewn tightly in the memory **quilt**[①] of our minds. We saw the continuing thread of life reflected in each other's eyes.

Then my daughter handed me a box. Inside was the essence of my mother the fragrance of another generation. I reached out to touch her legacy, opened the perfume bottle and **sprayed**[②], and she surrounded us.

① quilt [kwilt] n. 被状物，被子

② spray [sprei] v. 喷雾，喷射，扫射

父亲曾经送给她的很多玫瑰花。母亲非常钟爱红玫瑰，并且，玫瑰花也隐喻着发生在他们之间的一个故事：当初恋爱时，父亲曾经送给母亲一支玫瑰花，花茎很长，据说和父亲的身高一样长！最后，盒子里还有一瓶她最喜爱的埃莫罗德香水。令我难以置信的是，现在他们居然还在生产这种香水。尽管瓶身的形状变了，但那绿莹莹的颜色却是再也熟悉不过了。我朝着空气喷洒香水，飘渺的香气四溢，那一刻，我确信不疑，那就是母亲身上的气味。

我和女儿共同完成了这段心灵之旅，我们彼此在精神上也更加亲近了。通过爱的纽带，我们与一个逝去已久的生命——母亲，连结在一起；然而，我们也在内心深处细密地编织着属于自己的厚重记忆。在彼此眼中，我们看到了丝丝缕缕生命延续的光芒。

女儿随后将一只盒子交给我，里面保存着我母亲的特别气味，那是一种属于上一代人的香气。我伸手取出香水瓶，向四周喷洒。香气弥漫开来，恍惚之间，仿佛母亲一直就在我们身边，从未离去。

Dads Will Be Dads

父亲不可替代

◎ Susan M. Lang

While I was pregnant with my first child, **sweltering**[①] through the endless, fiery summer months in which ankles swelled and sweat poured forth profusely, I wanted only one thing: to give birth.

"I can't wait until this child is out," I would huff and puff in frustration.

My husband lovingly reassured me that the baby would spring forth at the appointed time. That some day I would be free from the burden of the added weight and the painful swollen ankles. I, however, felt as if the child had taken up permanent residence.

"Suppose the kid likes it in here and doesn't want to leave," I would say.

"Highly unlikely, dear. The baby will be here before you know it," he insisted, his feet still grounded firmly in reality, while mine were constantly elevated.

As it turned out, when my water broke that **fateful**[②] evening, I was shocked into reality. Our first daughter did leave the womb and enter the atmosphere. She even arrived three weeks early.

---

① sweltering ['sweltəriŋ] a. 酷热的

② fateful ['feitfəl] a. 宿命的；重大的，决定性的

美丽语录

I cannot think of any need in childhood as strong as the need for a father's protection.

—Sigmund Freud

我认为，一个孩子对父亲庇护的渴望比任何其他需求都要更强烈。

——西格蒙特·弗洛伊德

在我怀第一个孩子的时候，那是一个闷热而冗长的夏季，火热的天气似乎没有丝毫收敛的迹象。我的脚踝肿得高高的，身上总是大汗淋漓。我唯一想做的事情就是赶快把孩子生下来。

“我没法挨到孩子出生的时候了。”我满脸沮丧，愤怒地咆哮着。

我的丈夫深情地安慰我，说宝宝会顺利在预产期出生，到那时，脚踝的肿胀和疼痛自然就会消失，身体也不再那么臃肿沉重，我就可以摆脱负担获得解放了。而我却似乎觉得，孩子仿佛要在我的肚子里永久地待下去。

“那如果孩子喜欢待在肚子里，不打算出来呢？”我说。

“亲爱的，那是不可能的。孩子说不准在你没发觉的时候就出生了呢。”他语气坚定地说道，客观而理性，而我则明显有些失去理智。

后来，直到羊水破裂的那天晚上，我才从震惊中恢复理智，回到现实中来。我们的第一个女儿降生了，足足提前了三个星期。

When Mary was born, I was overjoyed. Not only was it a relief to hold her tiny body in my arms, but she was a red-headed beauty. Even when she was minutes old, I felt that we had a unique attachment. And we did, for she had been a part of me. However, what I didn't anticipate was how difficult it would be to let her go.

For those nine months that seemed like an eternity, the baby had been mine…all mine. She was joined with me and depended on only me for survival. Even though Tom could feel her kick through the **womb**[①] as she grew bigger, I usually had to notify him that she was moving. He depended on me to tell him what the baby was doing. The communication that Mary and I had was ours alone. Now, she was in the world and I had to share her with others. Including her dad.

Now, it's not that I didn't trust him. My husband is a compassionate husband and father. It's just that he doesn't do things the way that I do them.

He held the baby differently. I cradled her close, showing her my maternal love. He held her facing outward so she would have a world view. He transported her differently. I carried her in my arms from room to room as I tidied up. He placed her in the stroller and rolled her around so that he could put things away and still keep an eye on her. He comforted her differently. I rocked her quietly to calm her; he bounced her. He even fed her differently. I breast-fed her at 2:00 a.m. He bottle-fed her at 2:00 p.m. (Okay, so I can't hold biology against the poor guy.) It's just that it was difficult to accept that someone could relate to Mary in another way. Undoubtedly, I was very insecure, and sharing her was hard. Even with her dad.

Of course, there was the time that I was downstairs in the basement office

① womb [wu:m] n. 子宫；孕育处

女儿出生时，我高兴极了。不仅是因为我终于解脱了，可以用双臂把她小小的身体抱在怀里，而且她还是个有一头红发的小美女。尽管那时她才出生几分钟而已，但我就感觉到我和她之间有一种独特的情感，因为她曾经是我身体的一部分。但我当时并没有预料到，要我对她放手，这对我来说有多么艰难。

在看似无限漫长的怀孕的九个月里，宝宝是属于我的，完完全全只属于我自己。她来到我身体里，并依赖我生存下来。随着她在我的肚子里慢慢长大，我的丈夫隔着肚皮能感觉到她在里面踢来踢去，但是更多时候，他只能通过我知晓宝宝在肚子里的一举一动。女儿和我的交流只限于我们两人之间。但是，现在，她已经来到人世，我不得不与其他人，包括她爸爸，一起分享我们的女儿。

当然，这并不是我不信任他。他是一个极富爱心的丈夫和父亲。只是因为他做事情的方式与我不同而已。

他抱孩子的方法与我不同：我紧紧地怀抱着她，让她感受到我满腔的母爱；他总是把她脸朝外地抱着，让她看着这个新奇的世界。他带孩子走动的方式也不同：我会一边收拾屋子，一边把她抱在怀里，在不同的房间里走来走去；而他总是把她放在婴儿车里，推着她四处走，这样他可以空出双手而眼睛仍然盯牢孩子。他抚慰孩子的方式也很特别：我轻轻地摇着她让她安静下来，而他总是让她在他腿上不停地弹跳。甚至连他的喂养方法也不同：我在早上两点喂孩子吃母乳，他在下午两点喂孩子吃奶粉（好吧，也许我不该用男女不同的生理构造来反对这个可怜的家伙）。实际上，我只是很难接受有人能以某种方式与女儿联系在一起，毫无疑问，那是因为我很没有安全感。即使是与她的爸爸分享女儿，我也感到很难。

for a while working on a project. It was Dad's time to watch his little girl. As I reached the top of the steps after finishing my work, he asked, "Where's Mary?"

"What do you mean, where is Mary?" I screamed.

"I thought you had her," he said nonchalantly. "Don't worry, I'll find her." He had placed her on the living-room floor for a moment and then **inadvertently**[①] turned his back. We began our search there. As it turned out, she had crawled over to the floor-length picture window and was hiding behind the drapes. We found her giggling in delight at the birds on the front lawn and at the cars passing by. It was the first time that she had crawled. I seldom placed her on the floor, but Tom liked to give her room to stretch and play. No harm was done, in fact just the opposite. Our baby had reached a new point in her life because my husband, her dad, had let her expand her horizons.

During all those months of pregnancy while I complained, I never imagined how difficult it would be to let her go once she was born. For me, it was the first test of motherhood to let Dad be Dad. To realize that someone else could nurture my child in his own way. And to realize that what he had to give her, I couldn't give.

That is the beauty of parenting. That each mother and each father has a unique contribution. That our babies need the distinctive love and nurture that each one of us has to offer. And it pays off, too. By the time our second child was on the way, Mary was two years old. She and her dad had a wonderful relationship forged by the variety of experiences which they alone had shared.

After our youngest child, Kristi, arrived, I was able to give my husband more freedom and space in his distinctive parenting techniques. I, too, had grown. And, I had learned from his parenting style, even as he had learned from

① inadvertently [ˌinəd'vəːtəntli] ad. 不注意；疏忽地；非故意地

有一次，我待在地下室的工作间里做点事情，让她爸爸看着孩子。当我做完事情走上楼梯口时，他问我："女儿在哪里？"

"你什么意思？女儿不是应该和你在一起吗？"我尖叫起来。

"我以为她和你在一起，"他满不在乎地说，"别紧张，我会找到她的。"刚开始的时候，他把女儿放在客厅的地板上玩了一会儿，后来一不注意转过身去时，女儿就不见了。我们从客厅开始找起。原来，是她自己爬向落地窗边，躲到窗帘后面去了。我们找到她时，她正高兴地看着门前草坪上的小鸟，还有马路上驶过的汽车，不停地咯咯笑着。这是她第一次爬动。我很少把她放在地板上，但丈夫却总是喜欢给她更多的空间，让她自己去伸展手脚，尽情玩耍。他的做法并没有害处，相反，还大有好处。正因为我的丈夫，她的爸爸，让她自由地去扩展自己的视野，我们的女儿在她的生活道路上抵达了新的起点。

怀孕的那几个月里，我满腹抱怨，我很难想象，一旦她出生后，让我放手有多么困难。但是，这一次让爸爸照顾女儿的经历，正初次考验了我的母性。我逐渐意识到，别人也可以以他自己的方式来抚养孩子，而且她爸爸能给她的东西恰恰是我所无法给予的。

这就是为人父母的魅力所在。每个母亲和父亲对孩子都有自己独特的贡献，而孩子也需要父母双方各自提供不同的爱和培育。终于，功夫不负有心人，在我怀第二个孩子的时候，我们的女儿已经两岁了，她和爸爸相处得十分愉快。整个家庭其乐融融，因为他们俩分享了很多只属于他们自己的美好经历。

在我们最小的孩子克里斯蒂出生后，我渐渐能给我丈夫更多的自由空

mine. After all, we were a team.

"Well, they're all yours," I declared one day as I headed for the office.

"Aren't you just a little worried?" he teased.

"No, just remember to check behind the drapes if the baby disappears," I laughed. "Besides," I added, "you've got everything under control."

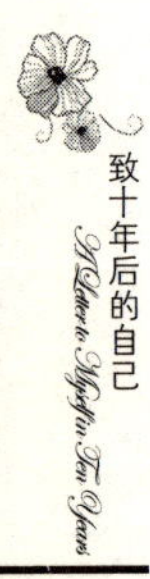

间，让他施展他独特的育儿方法。而且，我也变得成熟了，从他身上学到了很多；当然，他也从我这里学到很多。毕竟，我们同属一个“团队”。

“好吧，现在他们都归你了。”有一天，我走向工作室的时候说道。

“你不会有那么一点点担心吗？”他开玩笑地说。

“不会，不过如果孩子不见了，记得去窗帘后面找找。”我大笑起来，又说道，“还有，你已经可以独当一面了，不是吗？”

Romance Is in the Eyes of the Beholder

心中有爱，眼里才有爱

◎ Tina Runge

Life is so very busy. I think at times, we all get lost in the hustle and bustle of everyday life that we forget what it was that made us fall in love with our spouse or our significant other. Thankfully, I remembered.

My husband works hard. Many times his hours are long and his employment usually takes him away from the home front about one quarter of the year. I'm not complaining, mind you, because that was the same job that enabled me to be a stay-at-home mom and pursue my dream of writing. Yes, I'm a mother of three active boys and a published romance author. Naturally you'd think my life is full of romance. It is. My days consist of plotting and arranging the romantic lives of my characters so that the outcome is the proverbial "happily ever after". I love happily ever afters. This story is one of those.

I've never considered my husband of seventeen years to really be the romantic type. Sweet as he is, he isn't one to make dinner reservations at an **exclusive**[①] restaurant, or buy me a mushy, lovey-dovey card "just because". I do get flowers for all the proper occasions and the cards do come then, but is that really romantic? I never considered it to be, especially when the vast majority of

① exclusive [iks'klu:siv] a. 排外的，独占的；唯一的；完整的；奢华的

美丽语录

Seize the moments of happiness, love and be loved! That is the only reality in the world, all else is folly.

—Leo Tolstoy

抓住每一个快乐的瞬间，去爱与被爱吧！这是世界上唯一的事实，其他一切都是愚蠢的。

——列夫·托尔斯泰

生活总是太匆忙。有些时候，我们会迷失在这忙忙碌碌的庸常生活里，甚至遗忘了当初和我们的爱人是如何深深相爱的。幸好，我还记得。

我丈夫的工作很辛苦。他的工作时间总是很长，一年中大约四分之一的时间他都不在家，而在外面奔波忙碌着。当然，我并不是在抱怨，正是因为他的这份工作，才能让我做一个居家母亲，天天待在家里一边照顾孩子们，一边专心写作以实现我的写作梦想。没错，我是三个活泼好动的男孩的母亲，同时我还是一名写爱情小说的作家。很自然地，你会觉得，我在生活中一定经历了很多浪漫的爱情故事。的确如此。我每天的工作就是为我小说里的主人公们设计各种浪漫的情节，安排他们的爱情生活，并最后以俗话所说的“从此幸福地生活在一起”这样的美好结局而收场。我喜欢这种大团圆的结局，接下来我要讲的也是一个这样的故事。

我从未觉得相伴 17 年的丈夫是一个真正浪漫的人。尽管他对我很好，但他并不会去高级餐馆订餐，也不会给我买写着“只是因为”的那种情意绵绵的浪漫卡片。在一年四季各种节日里，他的确给我送过花，也写过祝

the rest of the female population was getting them, too. I had always wished for a little more...

One day, while I was working, several strange "incidences", for lack of a better word, crept into my mind. I was trying to concentrate on my current work-in-progress but "they" wouldn't leave me alone. "They" weren't any huge revelation or any spectacular plot points I could use for the rancher hero I was working on at the time, either.

They didn't have to do with the **elusive**① heroine I was still trying to get a grasp on. No. These were different, very different. They were about my husband. For some strange reason I couldn't get out of my head the last business trip he went on. He brought me back a pound of Ghirardelli malt balls and the romance novel I'd been meaning to buy. Then there was that fax I got that simply said, I love you. Could those two things fall under the romantic category? I decided they could. They most certainly should.

Other special moments flooded my mind as if a little keeper in my head had opened some "damn of memories". I remembered, vividly, the time my husband got the kids to bed early. No small feat, let me tell you! I was in the basement scrubbing a baseball uniform, wondering what made me angrier, those coaches who encouraged kids to slide when it was raining and muddy, or the league who purchased the white pants.

When I came up from finishing the chore, a scented bubble bath had been drawn, wine poured and candles lit. Has anyone ever been bathed by their spouse or significant other in an atmosphere like that? I can tell you firsthand that that was romantic! Those white baseball pants were soon forgotten and the coaches all forgiven. Then I fondly remembered another time, when the kids were at

---

① elusive [i'lu:siv] a. 难懂的；难捉摸的；难找的；逃避的

福卡片，但是，那就是浪漫吗？我从来没觉得这些就是所谓的浪漫，尤其考虑到大多数女性在节日里都会收到这样的礼物时，更是如此。我总是希望能有更特别一点的东西……

有一天，我正在写作，忽然有几件奇怪的“小事件”偷偷地溜进了我的脑海中。“小事件”，一时我找不到更好的词来形容，暂且就如此称呼它们吧。我努力地想集中精力继续手头的工作，但这些“小事件”却不让我清静。它们并不是什么伟大的发现，也不是什么令人惊叹的小说桥段，可以让我用在当时正在写的小说的农场男主人公身上。

它们跟我正在努力塑造但尚未成型的模糊的主人公没有丝毫关系。它们很特别，非常特别，因为它们关乎于我的丈夫。奇怪的是，丈夫上一次因公出差时做的一些事情总是挥之不去，在我的脑海里时不时地浮现出来。他给我带回 1 磅哥罗多利麦芽球，还有我一直想买的一本爱情小说。他还在出差途中给我发来了一份简单得不能再简单的传真——“我爱你”。这些能算是浪漫吗？我想应该算吧，毫无疑问，应该算。

我脑子里记忆的大门似乎顿时敞开了，其他一些特别的瞬间也如潮水般奔涌而来。我清晰地记得往日的一幕一幕，它们是如此生动，仿佛就在眼前。那可是一次不小的壮举，让我慢慢说给你听吧。那天，丈夫早早地哄孩子们上床睡觉了。我在地下室一遍又一遍地刷着孩子们的棒球服，心里不免愤愤然嘀咕着：那些教练为什么总是鼓励孩子们在下雨天泥泞的操场上摸爬滚打，让他们频频滑倒；而棒球联赛的组织者怎么会购买白色的棒球裤。

我做完杂活回到房间的时候，香气扑鼻的泡泡浴已经准备好了，周围点着蜡烛，红酒也摆在一旁。有人曾经享受过爱人给你准备的如此温馨的

Grandma's. My so-called unromantic hubby packed us both a sandwich and we rode bikes to the covered bridge in our town. We sat there, holding hands, eating and watching the geese and ducks. Just the two of us, just "being".

It hit me, then, as I stared at my computer monitor, the words "Ray loves Tina", endlessly floating across the screen.The screen saver was something else my sneaky husband had changed once before going out of town. How unfair I'd always been in my thinking. Was my husband romantic? Heavens, yes! I realized I could go on and on with those special moments, all the way back to when we first got married.

You may not think it's romantic for a man to travel on business with a container of deodorant that has his wife's picture taped to the front, or finding Hershey hugs and kisses that had been **strategically**[①] hidden all over the house because he wants you to know he misses you and is thinking about you while he's gone, but I sure do.

I know it's been said that beauty is in the eye of the **beholder**[②], but I think the same goes for romance. We all need to look for those special moments. And cherish them! I'm just thankful this romance author finally reflected and realized, again, what a hero she's married to!

① strategically [strə'ti:ʒikəli] ad. 战略上地；颇具策略地

② beholder [bi'həuldə] n. 旁观者

沐浴吗？我可以用我的亲身经历告诉你：那就是浪漫！白色的棒球裤很快就被忘记了，教练们也得到了我的原谅。我记得，还有一次，那时孩子们都在祖母家里。我所说的那个并不浪漫的丈夫，给我俩一人准备了一个三明治，然后我们一起骑车前往小镇上的一座小桥。我们坐在小桥边，手拉着手，吃着三明治，看着河里的鸭子和鹅。只有我们两个人，只是在一起静静地待着。

我回过神来，盯着电脑显示器，一串文字忽然跳了出来——“瑞爱蒂娜”，它不断地在屏幕上晃动飘浮。我被深深地打动了。一定是丈夫出门之前偷偷修改了屏幕保护程序的设置。而我总是沉浸在我自己的思维里，不曾发觉任何蛛丝马迹，这太不公平了。我的丈夫浪漫吗？天哪，这还用问吗？我发现，我可以一遍又一遍不停地回味所有这些美妙瞬间，一直回忆到我们刚刚结婚时的情景。

你可能觉得，丈夫出差时带着的除臭剂外壳上贴着妻子照片，这算不上浪漫；或者你可能觉得，妻子总是时不时在家里这个或那个地方发现丈夫精心藏好的“好时”巧克力，以此来表达他外出时对妻子一刻不停的思念，这也并没什么浪漫可言。但是，这一切，在我看来，就是浪漫，而且十足的浪漫。

心中有美，眼里才能看到美。我想，爱情也是一样的，心中有爱，眼里才能看到爱。我们都需要用心、用眼睛去寻找那些美好的瞬间，并好好珍惜它们。我很庆幸，我这个写爱情小说的作家，最终又一次意识到自己嫁给了一位多好的男主人公！

A Joy Forever
永远的玫瑰之约

◎ T. Jensen Lacey

John Keats wrote, "A thing of beauty is a joy forever." Perennial, enduring love is a thing of beauty, rather like a rose can be.

Every time I catch the scent of a rose, I think of enduring love. Being a **freelance**[1] journalist, years ago I had the pleasure of interviewing an elderly man. James Charlet had an interesting story, beginning two decades earlier when he lost his beloved wife, who had been a great lover of roses.

So deep was his grief when she died, so enduring was his love, that he asked his church if he could plant roses by the church walkway in his wife's memory. Of course, the priest there said yes.

James started with a few rose bushes. He planted lovely pinks, deep yellows and fragrant reds with names like "Yesterday" and "Golden Chersonese" and "Chrysler Imperial". The roses grew and **flourished**[2] under his never-ending care, for he also had retired and had a great deal of time on his hands.

He told me that those few roses didn't seem to be enough; they were insufficient to fully express his love for his wife. He asked the priest if he could

① freelance ['fri,la:ns] a. 自由择业的；兼职的

② flourish ['flʌriʃ] v. 茂盛；繁荣；挥舞；活跃

美丽语录

Love is the only bow on Life's dark cloud. It is the morning and the evening star.

—Robert G. Ingersoll

爱是生活的乌云下唯一的彩虹，是每个昼夜天际的明星。

——罗伯特·G. 英格索尔

诗人济慈写道："一件美好的事物会带来永恒的喜悦。"永恒耐久的爱情正是如此，它就是这样一件如玫瑰花般美好的事物。

每一次我闻到玫瑰的芳香，我就会联想到经得起岁月考验的爱情。几年前，我有幸作为自由撰稿人采访了一位名叫詹姆斯·夏洛特的老人。在他身上发生了--个有趣的故事，这个故事大约是从 20 年前他挚爱的妻子去世时开始的。他那位妻子非常喜爱玫瑰花。

妻子去世后，他悲痛万分，对妻子的爱非但没有丝毫减弱，却更加浓烈持久。于是，他请求教堂让他在教堂过道两旁种上玫瑰，以此来纪念他的妻子。牧师欣然同意了。

他种下了几丛玫瑰，有可爱的粉玫瑰，有深黄玫瑰，还有香气袭人的红玫瑰；玫瑰的名字也五花八门，叫"昨日重现""金色半岛""克莱斯勒帝王"等等。这些玫瑰花在他一刻不停的精心照料下长得又快又好，当然，这也是因为他退休了，有的是大把时间来伺弄这些花花草草。

他告诉我说，那几丛玫瑰似乎太少了，不足以表达他对死去的妻子的爱意。他请求牧师让他再多种些玫瑰。牧师又一次同意了。

plant some more roses; again, the priest said yes.

James planted some different kinds of roses this time: rare burgundies and hard-to-find violet roses, silver roses and hybrid roses created in the memory of others. Roses with names like "The Doctor" and "Alba Celeste" and "Honorable Lady Lindsay".

Still he was dissatisfied with what he called a paltry outward show of his inner feelings. He again approached the priest, asking if he could use part of the vacant lot next to the church that the church owned. Again, he was told yes.

James planted more roses and then went on to plant roses by the sidewalks up and down and around the entire city block, surrounding the church and grounds. Roses with names like "Red Meidiland" and "Trumpeter" and "Pikes Peak".

Now, rose bushes numbering in the hundreds are everywhere; the scent of them fills the air, the pied blooms catch the eye and blossoms float on the breeze along with the laughter of the children playing in the church playground. Couples strolling along downtown walk past the roses and instinctively take each other's hand. The altar-guild ladies cut great, fragrant bouquets of roses to decorate the church and altar, filling the interior with the color and perfume of love.

Decades after he began his project to honor his wife's memory, and years after I interviewed him about what he had done, James and I visited that rose garden one afternoon. The roses are tended now by someone hired by the church, as James is no longer able to care for them himself. So old and feeble is he now that his nurse and I half-carried him to the garden, helping him settle in his wheelchair in the midst of the blossoms. We sat under an arbor, one of his favorite places to sit in the hot summers when he'd been more vigorous.

I sat with him there in companionable silence, among the scent of a myriad

这次，他种了一些不同品种的玫瑰：稀有的勃艮第，罕见的紫罗兰玫瑰，银色玫瑰，还有各种杂交玫瑰。这些杂交玫瑰通常是用来纪念他人的，从他们的名字就可以看出来，比如“纪念医生”“阿尔巴·赛莱斯特”“尊敬的琳赛女士”等等。

但是，他仍不满意，他觉得这些玫瑰微不足道，并不能完全表达他的内心情感。他又去找牧师，请求牧师让他在教堂旁边那块空地上种满玫瑰。他又一次得到了肯定的答复。

他在空地上种下了更多的玫瑰，后来他继续在路边两侧都种上了玫瑰，最后教堂周边、整个街区都种上了他的玫瑰。玫瑰的品种也更多了，加入了“红色美德兰”“小号手”“皮克峰”等等。

现在，成百上千丛玫瑰遍布每个角落，浓郁的花香弥漫在空中，层层叠叠的各色花朵引人注目。微风吹过，玫瑰花瓣从空中婷婷袅袅地落下，在教堂空地上玩耍的孩子们发出阵阵爽朗的笑声。推着童车在街头散步的夫妇走过玫瑰花丛时，不禁下意识地握紧了对方的手。圣坛会的女士们剪下大把芬芳的玫瑰花束，用来装饰教堂和圣坛。教堂里面立刻充满了各种颜色的玫瑰，散发出阵阵爱的香气。

从他最初开始这项纪念他妻子的盛大工程，几十年已经过去了；而我上次采访他、了解他的故事之后，又过去了好几年。一天下午，我和老人一同来到了玫瑰园。这些玫瑰花现在已经由教堂雇佣专人打理，因为老人再也无法独自料理这些花儿了。现在他已经老了，十分虚弱，我和他的护士几乎是半抬着他进入玫瑰园的。我们在美丽的花丛中帮他坐到轮椅上，然后，我们在一棵大树底下坐了下来。那里曾是他精力尚好时在炎热夏天最爱坐的地方之一。

of rose blossoms. What was it that kept his love going inside him? What did the two of them have, even after one of them had died, that so many of us spend our lives desperately seeking?

It occurred to me then that some people are like **prisms**[1]: Anyone with a light in them can be near that person and have their light refracted into many different colors, like the colors of the roses around us. Prisms by themselves cannot make light, and light by itself cannot divide into the lovely colors of the rainbow. James Charlet's wife must have been like a prism, being there to magnify and refract her husband's light. He made her complete because she completed him. I thought at that moment how she must be smiling upon him, seeing all these gifts he had planted for her.

As I took his thin, old hand and saw him smile at me a bit sadly, in spite of the lovely midsummer day I found myself hoping that the love I have found is less ethereal than the scent of a rose, that it can endure as James's love has.

To nurture this love so it can endure throughout all our lives, even through the **infirmities**④[2] old age may bring, to care for one another and love one another even beyond the boundary that separates this existence from the next is my hope. Perhaps our love can remain as strong and as sweet as the roses that have endured and bloomed all these years, and be a thing of beauty, a joy forever.

① prism ['prizəm] n. 棱柱，棱镜；折光体

② infirmity [in'fə:miti] n. 虚弱，病身；疾病；弱点

我陪伴在他的身边，静静地坐着，无数玫瑰花瓣散发出的香气环绕着我们。是什么让爱在他内心持久留存？他们俩之间有什么呢，甚至在其中一方去世之后还永存不息？难道是我们中的很多人孤注一掷、追寻一生的东西？

我忽然想到，有些人就像棱镜一样，本身并不会发光，因此也无法折射出彩虹般绚丽丰富的色彩。但是，当一个内心能发光的人靠近他们时，他们就能把这缕光芒折射成各种不同的颜色，就如我们身边这些玫瑰般五彩斑斓。老人的妻子可能就是一枚棱镜，她总是可以放大、折射她丈夫的光芒。在他成全了她的同时，她也成全了他。我在想，那一刻，她一定看到了老人为她准备的礼物——这所有的玫瑰，她也一定在天堂向着老人微笑吧。

我握着他瘦削枯老的手，他向我微微笑着，眼神里不免有些伤感。尽管那是如此美丽的一个仲夏午后，我发现自己在心里默默祈祷着，但愿我所找到的爱情不要像玫瑰花香那么虚无缥缈，而能像老人的爱情那般持久隽永。

我也希望，我们能精心培育爱情，使其足以延续一生一世，哪怕年老体弱、满身病痛之时也不离弃；关爱彼此，纵然生死相隔，仍能始终不渝。也许，这样的话，我们的爱情，就能和这些玫瑰花一样经久不衰、繁盛绚丽，永远甜蜜、愉悦。

Melody

永不忘却的纪念

© Jennifer Koscheski

"Melody asked me to do this for her, and I said I would because I want her to be remembered well. But this is very difficult for me. There were thirteen months between us; she is in my memories as far back as they go, and I don't know how to live in a world without Melody in it." With these heartbroken words, and in a voice hoarse from weeping, I began my sister's **eulogy**①. For the next twenty minutes, I tried to explain to those in attendance how wonderful, good and worthy of life my sister was, and give them a glimpse of the void her death caused.

By all understanding of the bond, we were good sisters. Until our marriages we slept together, sharing our secrets in whispers and **giggles**② once the lights were out. We played often, fought sometimes and stuck together fiercely in school. We double-dated in high school, and she married first. We each had two sons and two daughters and poured ourselves into motherhood. Though our marriages forced us to live several states apart, we wrote often, and burned the phone lines between us with our calls because sometimes we just had to hear the

① eulogy ['juːlədʒi] n. 颂词；颂扬；悼词

② giggle ['gigl] v. 咯咯地笑

美丽语录

Life is a game and true love is a trophy.

—Rufus Wainwright

如果人生是一场比赛，那么真爱就是这场比赛的奖品。

——鲁弗斯·温赖特

“梅让我为她致悼辞，她说我肯定愿意，因为我希望人们能好好地记住她。但是，这对我来说非常困难。我们一起度过了她生命中最后的 13 个月。无论岁月怎样流转，她始终活在我的记忆深处，但我却不知失去了她以后，生活该如何继续。”我的声音因为哭泣而变得沙哑。说着这些令人心碎的话语，我开始为妹妹致悼辞。在接下来的 20 分钟里，我向在场的人们努力诉说着妹妹有多善良、多美好、多么应该继续活下去，也向他们倾诉妹妹的不幸离世给其他人的生活带来了多么莫大的空虚。

毋庸置疑，我们俩是极要好的姐妹。在结婚前，我们总是窝在一起睡觉；熄灯以后，我们窃窃私语着，分享彼此心中的秘密，有时也会咯咯大笑起来。我们经常一块儿玩，有的时候也会打起架来，但在学校时，我们却总是团结如一人。高中时，我们和各自的男朋友总是一起约会，但是她先结了婚。我们每人各有两儿两女，在孩子们身上我们倾注了所有的母爱。尽管婚姻使我们之间隔着几个州的距离，但我们经常通信，打电话煲电话粥。有的时候，我们打电话也只不过是想听听对方的声音。

other's voice.

I thought we knew all there was about being good sisters. Then she was diagnosed with cancer. Eleven months before she died she called and told me the dreadful news. The doctors gave her five years. She was scared, and I said I was, too, and we cried. We were not yet forty: How could we face separation in just five years? I still feel angry and cheated that we didn't get those other four years.

I determined to write her nearly every day and share every bit of the experience with her. I was with her often through the initial treatments, and there was a blissful three months in which no cancer could be found. Then suddenly the cancer returned with a **vengeance**①, terrifying in its rapid growth. Her first reaction, when the doctor told her, was to run. She did flee straight to me. We spent a week together praying, talking, crying and laughing. With everything in my soul fighting against the reality of her prognosis, I decided to embrace this horror with her, feeling every emotion, encouraging her in every step. I held her when she cried, and we mourned for the dreams we would never fulfill, the places we would never see together, the weddings she would miss and the grandchildren she would never hold. I promised her everything she asked for. We planned her daughters' weddings and talked of gifts she wanted her children to have. She listed all her personal belongings, and entrusted their distribution to me. She told me her deepest fears, confessed her shames and regrets, and shared her earnest longing for more time with her kids. During the day, I calmly listened to her, respecting her thoughts, completely **awed**② by her strength and dignity and faith. At night I wept bitterly.

I went to her home for two weeks after her visit, to help prepare for the

---

① vengeance ['vendʒəns] n. 报复；报仇

② awe [ɔ:] v. 使敬畏；使惊惧

我们是真正意义上的好姐妹。后来，她被诊断出患了癌症。从她打电话告诉我这个噩耗到她去世，中间仅仅隔了 11 个月。当时，医生告诉她存活期大概只有 5 年。她很恐惧，我说我也很害怕，两人大哭起来。那时我们还未满 40 岁：让我们如何面对 5 年之后残酷的生死别离？至今，我仍然对她仅活了一年而不是医生所说的 5 年耿耿于怀，感觉就像被欺骗了一样。

我下定决心每天给她写信，分享她的点滴感受和经历。在最初的治疗阶段，我经常陪着她。在大约三个月的时间里，很幸运地，没有在她体内发现癌细胞。然而，之后癌细胞突然卷土重来，并以骇人的速度迅速攀升。当医生告诉她这个消息时，她的第一反应是拔腿就跑，径直逃到我家中。在一个星期的时间里，我们待在一起，祈祷，聊天，哭泣，欢笑。尽管我内心深处始终难以接受她被诊断患有癌症这一事实，但我决定和她一起面对恐怖的病魔，去感受她的每一丝情感，在治疗的每个阶段给她鼓励。当她哭泣的时候，我会抱紧她；想起那些永远无法实现的梦想，那些无法一同前往的地方，那些她将会错过的婚礼，还有她永远无法拥抱的孙子孙女们，我们一起连声哀叹，唏嘘不已。我答应了她所要求的每件事。我们一起策划了她女儿们的婚礼，也讨论了她想要送给子女们的礼物。她列出了所有的个人财物，并委托我进行分配。她向我倾诉内心最深处的恐惧，坦白她的耻辱与悔恨，分享她最真诚的渴望——与孩子们再多待一些时日。白天，我平静地听她诉说。我尊重她的想法，并被她的坚强、尊严和信念完全折服。晚上的时候，我总是悲伤地流泪。

在她来我家住了一星期后，我去她家待了两个星期，帮她即将接受的

harsh chemical therapy plan about to be launched against her disease. When the day came for me to leave, my emotions were raw, the emotional intensity of our time together gripping me strongly. I was so afraid she would die during the treatments, and I wasn't nearly ready for it.

Taking her now-thin face in my hands, I whispered, "I don't know what to say."

Quietly, gently, she whispered back, "There are no more words, Jenn. We've already said them all."

I held her gently, as long as she could bear the pain of the embrace, trying to memorize for all time what she felt like. I cried the long drive home.

Weeks later the doctors reluctantly told us there was nothing more to be done. Other family members held back the report from Melody, fearful of causing her more pain by taking away all hope.

In simple words, for the morphine had **ravaged**[①] her senses, I explained it to her. My eyes were shining with tears, my throat closing on the words. Inexplicably, she said, "No tears." I choked them back, and we made plans for her to go home, where she most wanted to be. **Plaintively**[②], she told me she was afraid she would be alone at the final moment. I promised her I wouldn't let that happen.

Very early the next morning, I returned to the hospital, so we could be alone. Sitting as close to her as I could, holding her fragile hand, I asked her to please let me cry.

"Why?" she whispered.

"Because I'm going to miss you so much. I don't want you to die."

---

① ravage ['rævidʒ] v. 毁坏，破坏；掠夺

② plaintively ['pleintivli] ad. 可怜地；悲伤地

严酷化疗做些准备。离开她的那天，我们之间真挚的感情，以及我们在一起度过的美好时光，时时萦绕在我心头。她在治疗过程中随时都可能死去，对此，我并没有做好准备。我感到异常的恐惧。

我捧着她现在消瘦的脸，在她耳边轻轻说："我不知道该说点什么。"

她很平静，轻声回答道："简，不用说了。我们已经把要说的都说过了。"

我生怕我的拥抱弄疼了她，便很轻柔地抱着她，试图努力记住她每一个时刻的样子。那一次，我几乎是一路哭着开车回家的。

又过了几个星期，医生很不情愿地告知我们，他们已经尽力了。家人们向梅隐瞒了病情，因为他们害怕没有了希望，她会更加痛苦。

吗啡的药力破坏了她的感官，她总是昏昏沉沉的。我用寥寥数语向她说明了真相。我的双眼闪着晶莹的泪光，我的喉咙因为哽咽而几乎说不出话来。她含含糊糊地说道："别哭。"我努力抑制住自己，不让眼泪流下来。我们计划把她送回家，送回她现在最想去的地方。她很直白地告诉我说，她害怕在最后时刻来临时孤身一人。我向她保证，我会一直陪伴在她身边。

第二天清晨，很早的时候我就回到了医院，这样，我们就能独处一段时间。我握着她苍白无力的手，尽量坐得离她近一些。我请求她允许我哭一会儿。

"为什么？"她轻声地问。

"因为我会非常想念你。我不希望你死。"

我把头枕在她的床上，痛苦的热泪夺眶而出。她轻轻抚摸着我的头发，安慰着心中无比悲痛的我。那是一个异常痛苦的时刻。而后，我又重新找

Laying my head down on her bed, I wept hot, **anguished**[1] tears, while she stroked my hair and comforted me in my sorrow. It was an **agonizing**[2] moment. Later, I again found the strength to walk through it with her, but that morning for those minutes, I leaned on her, and she stood strong for me.

I had to go home. My family needed me, and the inevitable end had no definite date. Our mother stayed with Mel the last few weeks but called me on the last day and said to hurry, that the **hospice**[3] nurse was sure it would be within hours.

I dropped everything and made the trip as fast as I safely could, praying desperately that she could hang on till I got there. Mom told her I was coming, though she was doubtful Melody understood. Walking in the door of her room, I was weak with relief that I had made it in time. For ninety-eight minutes I talked to my sister, prayed over her, kissed her, sang to her and read aloud all her favorite scriptures. She never spoke, but I know she heard me. The nurse was amazed she hung on for so many hours with a 107-degree fever, only four respirations a minute and almost no blood pressure.

I will always believe she waited for me.

This is the part of sisterhood I'm still learning: going on after a sister is no longer there. The pain and loss are worse than I imagined, and time without her stretches before me in aching loneliness.

I'm at peace in knowing she is with Christ, but as our older sister said bitterly to a well-meaning friend who tried to comfort her at the funeral, "Heaven would have been just as beautiful thirty years from now."

My memories are indescribably precious. I have no regrets; we wasted

---

① anguished ['æŋgwiʃt] a. 很痛苦的

② agonizing ['ægənaiziŋ] a. 苦恼的；痛苦难忍的

③ hospice ['hɔspis] n.（宗教团体等办的）旅客住宿处；（晚期病人）护理所

回了陪她一起度过难关的勇气。但是，在那几分钟里，我依偎着她，她成了我坚强的精神支柱。

后来，因为家人需要我，我不得不赶回家去。毕竟，虽然结局不可避免，但最终时间并不确定。在最后几个星期里，母亲陪伴在妹妹身边。最后一天，母亲打电话给我，让我尽快赶到，因为负责临终关怀的护士肯定她剩下的时间不多了，几个小时而已。

我立刻扔下一切，以能保证安全的最快速度飞奔过去，绝望地祈祷她能坚持下去直到我赶到。尽管并不确定她是否能听懂，但是母亲告诉她，我来了。我快步走进病房，能够及时赶到让我放松下来，也让我倍感虚弱。在这 98 分钟的时间里，我跟她说话，为她祈祷，亲吻她，为她歌唱，大声朗读她最喜爱的文字。她一言不发，但我知道她听得见。护士很惊讶，她居然在发着 107 度的高烧、一分钟仅呼吸 4 次，而且几乎没有血压的情况下坚持了那么久。

我总觉得那是因为她在等我。

好姐妹去世后如何继续生活，这是我在姐妹感情方面仍需学习的崭新一课。那种痛苦和失落远比我想象的要糟糕得多。人生的漫漫长路没有她的陪伴，徒留我一人在痛苦中孤独前行。

她此刻与上帝同在，对这一点我感到很欣慰。葬礼上，一位好心的朋友想要安慰我们的大姐，大姐伤心地说："从现在开始，往后的 30 年里，天堂将会因为有了梅而始终美丽。"

我的回忆弥足珍贵。我没有任何遗憾；我们没有浪费时间，曾一起面

no time, faced the dreadful future together, said all the right words, smiled and laughed and cried in complete **unison** ⑩ [1], all the way up to the last moment possible. She was a perfect sister.

A few weeks ago her eighteen-year-old daughter, Melissa, called me, sobbing with grief. "Aunt Jenn, I'm afraid everyone is going to forget how wonderful Mama was." Weeping with her, I promised that wouldn't happen. I won't let her be forgotten.

① unison ['ju:nizn] n.（做事、说话）一起，一致行动；（歌唱或演奏）齐声

对可怕的明天，说完了所有该说的话，不约而同地放声大笑、失声痛哭，一直到那最后一刻。她是我最好的姐妹。

几个星期前，她 18 岁的女儿梅丽莎打电话给我。在电话那头，她伤心地哭了起来。“简姨，恐怕现在每个人都已经开始忘记妈妈有多好了。”我忍不住和她一起流泪。我向她承诺过她担心的事不会发生，因为我永远不会将她遗忘。

Chapter 2

勇于活在当下

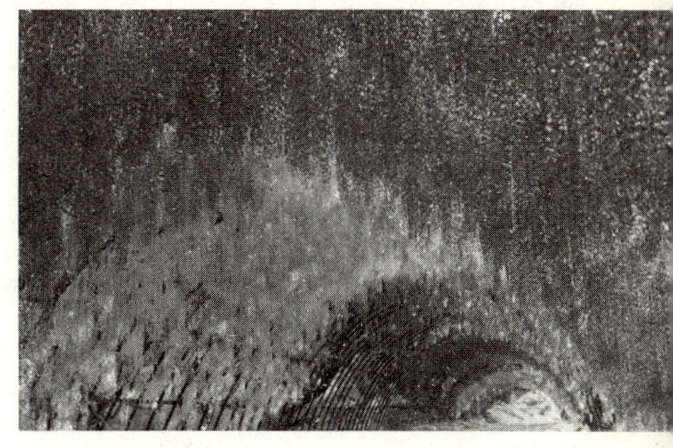

Life consists not in holding good cards but in playing those you hold well

—— Josh Billings

人生不在于手握一副好牌，而是打好你手上的牌。

——乔希·比林斯

A Place to Stand

收费员的美好生活

◎ Charles Garfield

If you have ever gone through a toll booth, you know that your relationship to the person in the booth is not the most **intimate**[1] you'll ever have. It is one of life's frequent nonencounters: You hand over some money; you might get change; you drive off.

Late one morning in 1984, headed for lunch in San Francisco, I drove toward a booth. I heard loud music. It sounded like a party. I looked around. No other cars with their windows open. No sound trucks. I looked at the toll booth. Inside it, the man was dancing.

"What are you doing?" I asked.

"I'm having a party," he said.

"What about the rest of the people?" I looked at the other toll booths.

He said, "What do those look like to you?" He pointed down the row of toll booths.

"They look like...toll booths. What do they look like to you?"

He said, "Vertical coffins. At 8:30 every morning, live people get in. Then

---

① intimate ['intimeit] a. 亲密的；私人的；关系紧密的

美丽语录

My secret to a long, healthy life is to always keep working. It keeps me busy and happy, and gives me a reason to stay alive.

—Johannes Heesters

我长寿健康的秘诀在于总是不停工作，它给予我忙碌和愉悦，并给了我一个继续生活的理由。

——约翰内斯·黑丝特斯

如果你曾开车通过收费站，你就了解收费员与你的关系可谈不上密切；他不过是我们生活中遇到的众多陌生人中的一员：你递给他一些钱，他找你零钱，然后你便驾车离去。

1984 年的某天上午晚些时候，我驾车前往旧金山去吃午餐。途中经过一个收费站时，我听见阵阵音乐声，音量开得很大，听上去像是在开派对。我伸出头去四处张望，没看见别的车开着窗户，也没见有广播车经过。我看了看收费亭，原来里面有个人在跳舞。

“你在干什么？”我问。

“我在开派对。”他说。

“那么其他人呢？”我看着其他收费亭。

他用手指着一整排收费亭，说道：“你觉得它们看起来像什么？”

“它们看起来像……收费亭啊。你怎么看？”

他说：“它们像一个个竖起来摆放的棺材。每天早晨 8:30，活人走进去。然后，他们在接下去的 8 个小时里变成死人。下午 4:30 的时候，他们像拉撒路一样死而复生，他们又活过来，回家去了。在那 8 个小时里，他

they die for eight hours. At 4:30, like Lazarus from the dead, they reemerge and go home. For eight hours, brain is on hold, dead on the job. Going through the motions."

I was amazed. This guy had developed a philosophy, a **mythology**[①] about his job. Sixteen people dead on the job, and the seventeenth, in precisely the same situation, figures out a way to live. I could not help asking the next question: "Why is it different for you? You're having a good time."

He looked at me. "I knew you were going to ask that. I don't understand why anybody would think my job is boring. I have a corner office, glass on all sides. I can see the Golden Gate, San Francisco, and the Berkeley hills. Half the Western world vacations here and I just **stroll**[②] in every day and practice dancing."

① mythology [mi'θɔlədʒi] n. 神话；神话学；神话集

② stroll [strəul] v. 闲逛；漫步

们的脑子停滞了，像死人一样机械地重复着工作时仅有的几个动作。”

我很惊讶，这个收费员自己想出了一套哲学，或者说有关工作的一则神话。16 个人在工作时死去，还有另外第 17 个人，处于完全相同的境况，却想出了活过来的方法。我忍不住问他：“你为什么如此特别呢？你看起来很享受工作，过得很愉快嘛。”

他看着我，说道：“我就知道你会这么问。我不明白为什么每个人都觉得我的工作很枯燥。我有一间角落里的办公室，四周都是玻璃窗，能看见金门海峡、旧金山，也能看见伯克利山。西方世界的很多人都前来此处观光度假，而我则每天漫步走入办公室，练习舞步呢。”

What Really Matters in Life
生活中最重要的东西

◎ Jennifer Keitt

A vacationing American businessman was standing on the pier of a quaint coastal fishing village in southern Mexico when a small boat with just one young fisherman pulled into the dock. Inside the small boat were several large yellowfin tuna. The American complimented the Mexican on the quality of his fish.

"How long did it take you to catch them?" the American **casually**① asked.

"Oh, a few hours," the Mexican replied.

"Why don't you stay out longer and catch more fish?" the American businessman then asked.

The Mexican warmly replied, "With this I have more than enough to support my family's needs."

The businessman then became serious, "But what do you do with the rest of your time?"

Responding with a smile, the Mexican fisherman answered, "I sleep late, play with my children, watch ball games, and take **siesta**② with my wife. Sometimes in the evenings I take a stroll into the village to see my friends, play

---

① casually ['kæʒjuəli] ad. 偶然地，随便地，漫不经心地

② siesta [si'estə] n. 午睡

美丽语录

It is not the place, nor the condition, but the mind alone that can make anyone happy or miserable.

决定人之苦乐的不是地点，也不是环境，而是思想。

墨西哥南部一个古朴的沿海小渔村，一位正在度假的美国商人站在码头上。这时，一名年轻渔民拖着一艘小船拉进了岸边码头。小船上有几条很大的黄鳍金枪鱼。美国商人向渔民恭维了几句，夸他的鱼质量真不错。

“你花了多长时间捕到这些鱼的？”美国人随意地问道。

“哦，几个小时吧。”墨西哥人回答。

“你为什么不在海上多待一会儿，再多捕点鱼呢？”美国商人又问。

墨西哥人热情地回答说：“我捕的这些鱼养家糊口绰绰有余了。”

商人变得严肃起来，“那你剩下的时间都做什么？”

墨西哥渔民欣然一笑，回答说：“我会睡个懒觉，和我的孩子们玩耍，看看球赛，和我妻子睡个午觉。晚上的时候，有时我会漫步到村子里，见见朋友，弹弹吉他，唱唱歌……”

the guitar, sing a few songs..."

The American businessman impatiently interrupted, "Look, I have an MBA from Harvard, and I can help you to be more profitable. You can start by fishing several hours longer every day. You can then sell the extra fish you catch. With the extra money, you can buy a bigger boat. With the additional income that larger boat will bring, you can then buy a second boat, a third one, and so on, until you have an entire fleet of fishing boats.

"Then, instead of selling your catch to a middleman you'll be able to sell your fish directly to the processor, or even open your own cannery. Eventually, you could control the product, processing and **distribution**[①]. You could leave this tiny coastal village and move to Mexico City, or possibly even LA or New York City, where you could even further expand your enterprise."

Having never thought of such things, the Mexican fisherman asked, "But how long will all this take?"

After a rapid mental calculation, the businessman pronounced, "Probably about 15-20 years, maybe less if you work really hard."

"And then what, senor?" asked the fisherman.

"Why, that's the best part!" answered the businessman with a laugh. "When the time is right, you would sell your company stock to the public and become very rich. You would make millions."

"Millions? Really? What could I do with it all?" asked the young fisherman in disbelief.

The businessman boasted, "Then you could happily retire with all the money you've made. You could move to a quaint coastal fishing village where you could sleep late, play with your grandchildren, watch ballgames, take siesta

① distribution [ˌdistri'bju:ʃən] n. 分布；分发，分配；散布；销售量

美国商人不耐烦地打断了他的话，“你看，我从哈佛毕业，有工商管理硕士学位，我能帮你赚到更多的钱。听着，最初时，你可以每天多花几个小时捕鱼，然后出售多捕的鱼。用卖鱼的钱，你可以买一艘更大的船，这艘船能给你带来更丰厚的收入，然后你就可以买第二艘船，第三艘船，越来越多。最后，你会发现自己已经变得非常富有，拥有一整支捕鱼船队了。”

“再往后，你就不用把你的鱼卖给中间商，而是直接把鱼卖给加工厂，或者干脆自己办一个罐头工厂。最后，你可以控制鱼类加工和销售整个链条。你可以离开这个小渔村，搬到墨西哥城，或者洛杉矶、纽约，在那里进一步扩大你的企业。”

墨西哥渔民从未想过这些，他问：“但是，这得花多久啊？”

商人快速地在脑子里计算了一遍，宣布道：“可能需要 15—20 年左右。如果你足够努力，也许不用那么久。”

“先生，那然后呢？”渔民问。

“哎呀，这就是最精彩的部分呀！”商人大笑起来。“如果时机合适，把公司股票卖给公众，你就能变得非常富有，成为百万富翁了。”

“百万富翁？真的吗？那么多钱做什么用呢？”年轻渔民半信半疑地问。

商人引以为豪地说道：“然后你就可以带着巨额财富愉快退休了。你可以搬到一个古朴的海边小渔村。你可以睡懒觉，和孩子们玩耍，看看球赛，和妻子睡个午觉。晚上的时候，漫步走进村子里，和朋友弹弹吉他，唱唱

with your wife, and stroll to the village in the evenings where you could play the guitar and sing with your friends all you want."

The **moral**① of the story is: Know what really matters in life, and you may find that it is already much closer than you think

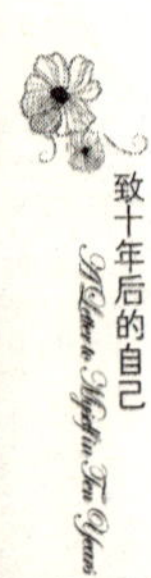

① moral ['mɔrəl] n. 寓意；道德，品行，伦理

歌，做任何你想做的事。”

这个故事的寓意在于：懂得生活中什么是真正重要的东西，然后你会发现实际上它们就在眼前，比你想象的要离你近得多。

Finding Copper Pennies
铜币与人生

◎ Anonymous

There was a small boy who when walking down the street one day found a bright copper penny. He was so excited that he found money and it didn't cost him anything. This experience led him to spend the rest of his days walking with his head down, eyes wide open, looking for treasure.

During his lifetime he found 296 pennies, 48 nickels, 19 dimes, 16 quarters, 2 half dollars and one **crinkled**[①] dollar bill. For a total of $13.96.

He got money for nothing. Except that he missed the breathless beauty of 31,369 sunsets, the colorful **splendor**[②] of 157 rainbows, the fiery beauty of hundreds of maples nipped by autumn's frost. He never saw white clouds drifting across blue skies, shifting into various **wondrous**[③] formations. Birds flying, sun shining, and the smiles of a thousand passing people are not a part of his memory.

Who do you know that is living like this? Head is bent down burdened with trivial things afraid of pain and criticism and fear of things that never happen hoping to find that copper penny...for nothing.

---

① crinkle ['kriŋkl] v. 变皱；沙沙作响

② splendor ['splendə] n. 光辉，壮丽；显赫；辉煌

③ wondrous ['wʌndrəs] a. 令人惊奇的；非常的

美丽语录

Those who are not looking for happiness are the most likely to find it, because those who are searching forget that the surest way to be happy is to seek happiness for others.

—Martin Luther King

不刻意为自己寻找快乐的人最有可能找到快乐，因为寻快乐的人忘记了快乐的捷径在于为他人寻求快乐。

——马丁·路德·金

一天，有位小男孩走在街上，无意之间捡到了一枚铜币。他很兴奋，因为他不费吹灰之力就得到了意外之财。有了这次经历后，在接下来的大半天时间里，他开始压低头、睁大眼睛，不停地沿街搜寻着。

在他的一生中，他一共捡到了 296 枚 1 分硬币，48 枚 5 分镍币，19 枚 10 分银币，16 枚 25 分硬币，2 张 50 分纸币以及 1 张残破的 1 元纸币，合计共 13.96 美元。

的确，为了这些金钱，他没有付出任何代价。但是，他错过了 31,369 次美丽得让人窒息的日出，157 次五彩斑斓、光辉壮丽的彩虹，成千上万秋霜尽染中火红炽热的美丽枫叶。他从未留意蔚蓝的天际，朵朵洁白的云儿转瞬变幻，组成一幕幕让人惊叹的奇观；他也不会记得，空中自由的飞鸟，天上夺目的太阳，还有匆匆行人那会心的微笑。

你知道有谁是这样生活着的吗？他们拘泥于日常琐事，对痛苦、批评充满了恐惧，常常杞人忧天，负担沉重，总是弯着腰低下头，希望不费吹灰之力就能找到人生的宝藏。

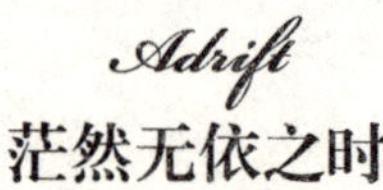

茫然无依之时

© Adam Khan

In 1982 Steven Callahan was crossing the Atlantic alone in his sailboat when it struck something and sank. He was out of the shipping lanes and floating in a life raft, alone. His supplies were few. His chances were small. Yet when three fishermen found him seventy-six days later (the longest anyone has survived a shipwreck on a life raft alone), he was alive—much **skinnier**[①] than he was when he started, but alive.

His account of how he survived is fascinating. His **ingenuity**[②]—how he managed to catch fish, how he fixed his solar still (**evaporates**[③] sea water to make fresh) —is very interesting.

But the thing that caught my eye was how he managed to keep himself going when all hope seemed lost, when there seemed no point in continuing the struggle, when he was suffering greatly, when his life raft was **punctured** ④[④] and after more than a week struggling with his weak body to fix it, it was still leaking air and wearing him out to keep pumping it up. He was starved. He was

---

① skinny ['skini] a. 皮的；皮包骨头的

② ingenuity [,indʒi'nju:iti] n. 心灵手巧；独创性；精巧

③ evaporate [i'væpəreit] v. 蒸发，失去水分；消失

④ puncture ['pʌŋktʃə] v. 刺穿；削弱

美丽语录

Ordinary people believe only in the possible. Extraordinary people visualize not what is possible or probable, but rather what is impossible. And by visualizing the impossible, they begin to see it as possible.

— Cherie Carter Scott

平凡者只相信可能的，非凡者想象的不是可能或较可能的，而是不可能的。借由想象不可能，他们开始视之为可能。

——雪莉·卡特·史考特

1982年，史蒂文·卡拉翰驶着帆船独自横渡大西洋时，帆船撞沉了。他偏离了航道，在一艘救生艇上独自一人随着海浪漂浮。食物和水已经所剩不多，他生还的希望十分渺茫。然而，76天（从海难中幸存下来、独自在救生艇上生活的最长时间记录）后，当三位渔民发现他时，他居然还活着，虽然瘦得只剩下了皮包骨头，但总算还活着。

他对自己如何幸存下来的描述非常引人入胜。他是如何利用聪明才智成功地捕鱼，怎样修好他的太阳能蒸馏器（用于蒸馏海水以获得淡水），这是个非常有趣的故事。

但是，最吸引我的在于，在所有希望均告破灭的时候，在受尽折磨、一切努力看似毫无意义的时候，在救生艇被刺穿、费尽力气修了一个多星期还是漏气的时候，在给救生艇打气几乎耗尽了最后一丝气力的时候，他是如何成功地让自己继续活下去的。他极度饥饿，脱水严重，精疲力竭。放弃在当时看起来是唯一理性的选择。

desperately **dehydrated**[1]. He was thoroughly exhausted. Giving up would have seemed the only sane option.

When people survive these kinds of circumstances, they do something with their minds that gives them the courage to keep going. Many people in similarly desperate circumstances give in or go mad. Something the survivors do with their thoughts helps them find the guts to carry on in spite of overwhelming odds.

"I tell myself I can handle it," wrote Callahan in his narrative. "Compared to what others have been through, I'm fortunate. I tell myself these things over and over, building up **fortitude**[2]..."

I wrote that down after I read it. It struck me as something important. And I've told myself the same thing when my own goals seemed far off or when my problems seemed too overwhelming. And every time I've said it, I have always come back to my senses.

The truth is, our circumstances are only bad compared to something better. But others have been through much worse. I've read enough history to know you and I are lucky to be where we are, when we are, no matter how bad it seems to us compared to our fantasies. It's a sane thought and worth thinking.

So here, coming to us from the extreme edge of survival, are words that can give us strength. Whatever you're going through, tell yourself you can handle it. Compared to what others have been through, you're fortunate. Tell this to yourself over and over, and it will help you get through the rough spots with a little more fortitude.

---

① dehydrate [di:'haidreit] v. 脱水；去水

② fortitude ['fɔ:titju:d] n. 刚毅，坚毅，不屈不挠

人们在这样的以及类似的情况中幸存下来，是与他们的精神分不开的，精神赋予了他们勇气继续活下去。很多人在类似的绝望境地中选择放弃或者变得疯狂。幸存者们正是因为尚存的理智，才能鼓起勇气继续活下去，尽管情况极端不利。

“我告诉自己，我一定能挺过去。”卡拉翰在他的叙述中写道。“与其他人经历的苦难相比，我算是幸运的。我一遍又一遍地对自己说着这些来增强自己的毅力……”

读到这段话后，我把它当做重要的东西记录下来，因为它深深地震撼了我。当我的目标看起来遥不可及时，当我的问题看起来堆积如山时，我总是告诉自己同样的话，而且每一次我对自己这么说时，我总能恢复理智。

事实上，我们的境况之所以看起来很糟，是因为我们总是把它与更好的境况相比较。但是，别人可能遭遇过更糟糕的情况。我读过很多历史书，因此也了解，无论我们所处的境况与想象相比有多么糟糕，我们还是应该庆幸我们所处的时代和所在的国家。这是一个理智的想法，也值得我们深思。

因此，从追求幸存的极度边缘感受中，我们能得到一些赋予我们力量的信念。无论正在经历什么，告诉你自己一定能挺过去。与他人的经历相比，你是幸运的。一遍又一遍地告诉自己这些，它就能帮助你以更坚强的毅力度过一个又一个难关。

Three Words of Wisdom: "Don't We All?"

我们不都需要帮助吗?

◎ Anonymous

One evening I was parked in front of the mall wiping off my car. I had just come from the car wash and was waiting for my wife to finish work.

Coming my way from across the parking lot, was what society would consider a **bum**[①]. From the looks of him he had no car, no home, no clean clothes and no money. There are times when you feel generous, but there are times that you just don't want to be bothered. This was one of the don't-want-to-be-bothered times!

"Hope he doesn't ask me for money," I thought.

He didn't. He came and sat on the curb in front of the bus stop and he didn't look like he could have enough money to even ride the bus.

After a few minutes he spoke. "That's a very nice car," he said. He was **ragged**[②], but had an air of dignity around him.

I said "Thanks", and continued wiping off my car.

He sat there quietly as I worked. The expected plea for money never

---

① bum[bʌm] n. 流浪汉，游荡者，懒鬼

② ragged['rægid] a. 衣衫褴褛的，粗糙的，刺耳的，(外形)不规则的，不完美的

美丽语录

God helps those who help themselves.

—Algernon Sidney

天助自助者。

——阿尔吉农·西德尼

一天傍晚，我把刚洗过的车停在购物中心门前，一边擦拭车身的水渍，一边等妻子下班。

从我站的位置看过去，在停车场的另一头，站着一个会被社会称作“流浪汉”的人。从外表看，他一贫如洗，无家可归，衣衫污浊，更别说有自己的车了。遇到如此情景，有时你会慷慨解囊，但有时你根本不想予以理睬。那时，我就想置之不理，继续擦着我的车。

“希望他不会向我要钱。”我想。

他没有向我伸手要钱。他走过来，在公交车站前的路沿上坐下来。他似乎连坐公交车的钱也没有。

过了几分钟，他开口说话了，“车子不错啊。”他说。尽管他衣衫褴褛，但他却有种威严的神态。

我说了声“谢谢”，然后继续擦我的车。

就在我擦车的时候，他安静地在一旁坐着，并没有如我预想的那样过来要钱。我们之间的气氛变得越发安静了。一个声音从我心底响起：“去问

came. As the silence between us widened, something inside said, "Ask him if he needs any help." I was sure that he would say yes, but I held true to the inner voice.

"Do you need any help?" I asked.

He answered in three simple, but profound, words that I shall never forget. We often look for wisdom in great accomplishments. I expect it from those of higher learning and accomplishments. I expected nothing here but an outstretched grimy hand.

Then, he spoke three words that shook me. "Don't we all?" he said.

I needed help. Maybe not for bus fare or a place to sleep, but I needed help. I reached in my wallet and gave him not only enough for bus fare but enough to get a warm meal and shelter for the day.

Those three little words still ring true. No matter how much you have, no matter how much you have accomplished, we all need help.

No matter how little you have, no matter how loaded you are with problems, even without money or a place to sleep, you can give help. Even if it's just a compliment, you can give that!

You never know when you may see someone that appears to have it all, yet in actuality they need you to give them what they don't have—a different perspective on life, a glimpse of something beautiful, a respite from daily **chaos** ③ [1]—that only you, through a torn world can see.

Maybe the man was just a homeless stranger wandering the streets. Maybe he was more than that. Maybe he was sent by a power that is great and wise to minister to a soul too comfortable in himself.

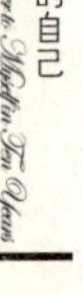

---

① chaos['keiɔs] n. 混乱，无秩序，混沌

问他是否需要帮助。”我确信他肯定会说需要，但是我还是选择忠于我内心的呼声。

“你需要什么帮助吗？”我问道。

他没有伸出肮脏的双手向我乞讨，他只回答了短短一句。这简单但却很深刻的一句话，让我永生难忘。这样的回答，我原以为只能来自学识渊博、成就卓著的人们，因为我们经常试图从伟大的成就中汲取智慧的养分，却没曾想到从他的口中说了出来。

他说：“我们每个人不都需要帮助吗？”这句话深深震撼了我。

是的，我需要帮助，可能我需要的不是坐公交车的钱，也不是睡觉的地方，但我的确需要帮助。我把手伸进钱包，给了他一些钱。这些钱不仅能让他坐得起公交车，也够他吃顿热饭，找个地方美美地睡一觉。

这句话至今仍言犹在耳，听上去十分真实。无论你拥有多少，也无论你成就了多少，我们都需要帮助。

无论你多么渺小，无论你身上背负多少问题，甚至一文不名，流离失所，你仍然能帮助他人，哪怕只是一句赞美的话——这都是你能给予的！

你永远不知道，有些人的生活看起来近乎完美，什么也不缺，然而，实际上他们需要你给予一些他们没有的东西，可能是看待生活的不同视角，也可能是发现美丽的惊鸿一瞥，又或者是远离日常喧嚣的片刻宁静。而所有这一切，只有你透过这个支离破碎的世界才能发现。

也许这个人不过是个浪迹街头、无家可归的陌生人。也许他还有更复

Maybe someone looked down, called an angel, dressed him like a bum, and then said, “Go minister to that man cleaning the car; that man needs help.”

Don’t we all?

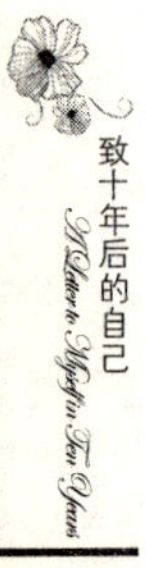

杂的身份。又或许他是伟大而明智的力量派来照料他自己过于闲适安逸的灵魂。

或许神从天堂往人间看了看，叫了一名天使，让他打扮成流浪汉的模样，然后说："去照顾一下那个擦洗车子的人吧，他需要帮助。"

我们不都需要帮助吗?

The Cab Ride I'll Never Forget

难忘的出租车之旅

◎ Kent Nerburn

Twenty years ago, I drove a cab for a living. One time I arrived in the middle of the night for a pick up at a building that was dark except for a single light in a ground floor window.

Under these circumstances, many drivers would just **honk**① once or twice, wait a minute, then drive away. But I had seen too many **impoverished**② people who depended on taxis as their only means of transportation. Unless a situation smelled of danger, I always went to the door. This passenger might be someone who needs my assistance, I reasoned to myself. So I walked to the door and knocked.

"Just a minute," answered a **frail**③, elderly voice.

I could hear something being dragged across the floor. After a long pause, the door opened. A small woman in her 80's stood before me. She was wearing a print dress and a pillbox hat with a veil pinned on it, like somebody out of a 1940s movie. By her side was a small nylon suitcase.

---

① honk [hɔːŋk] v.（使）雁叫；鸣（汽车喇叭）

② impoverished [im'pɔvəriʃt] a. 贫困的，赤贫的；耗竭的

③ frail [freil] a. 脆弱的；虚弱的

美丽语录

The mystery of life is not a problem to be solved; it is a reality to be experienced.

—Jacobus Johannes Leeuw

生活的奥秘并不是一个需要解决的问题，而是一种需要人们去经历的现实。

——雅各布斯·约翰内斯·莱乌

20 年前，我是一名出租车司机。一天深夜，我驾车前往一处房子去接客人。到达时，房子里漆黑一片，只有底层一扇窗里透出一盏灯的光亮。

在这样的情况下，很多司机只会鸣一两次喇叭，等上几分钟，然后就驱车离去。但我见过很多贫穷的人们，他们依赖出租车作为唯一的交通工具。除非我感觉情况危险，否则我总是会走上门去。我心里想，这位乘客有可能需要我的帮助，于是，我走到门前，敲了敲门。

“稍等片刻。”一个虚弱而苍老的声音回答道。

我能听见什么东西在地板上拖曳的声音。又过了很长时间，门打开了。一位 80 多岁的小个子老太太站在我面前。她身穿一件印花裙，头戴一顶别有面纱的小圆帽，仿佛从 20 世纪 40 年代的老电影里走出来似的。她的身边有只尼龙手提箱。

The apartment looked as if no one had lived in it for years. All the furniture was covered with sheets. There were no clocks on the walls, no knickknacks or utensils on the counters. In the corner was a cardboard box filled with photos and glassware.

"Would you carry my bag out to the car?" she said. I took the suitcase to the cab, then returned to assist the woman. She took my arm and we walked slowly toward the curb. She kept thanking me for my kindness.

"It's nothing," I told her. "I just try to treat my passengers the way I would want my mother treated."

"Oh, you're such a good boy," she said. When we got in the cab, she gave me an address, then asked, "Could you drive through downtown?"

"It's not the shortest way," I answered quickly.

"Oh, I don't mind," she said. "I'm in no hurry. I'm on my way to a hospice."

I looked in the rear view mirror. Her eyes were glistening.

"I don't have any family left," she continued. "The doctor says I don't have very long."

I quietly reached over and shut off the meter. "What route would you like me to take?" I asked.

For the next two hours, we drove through the city. She showed me the building where she had once worked as an elevator operator. We drove through the neighborhood where she and her husband had lived when they were newlyweds. She had me pull up in front of a furniture warehouse that had once been a ballroom where she had gone dancing as a girl.

Sometimes she'd ask me to slow in front of a particular building or corner and would sit staring into the darkness, saying nothing.

这座公寓看起来似乎已经多年无人居住了。所有家具都用被单盖着，墙上没有挂时钟，柜子上也没有摆放装饰品和器皿。房子一角有一只纸箱，里面装满了照片和各式玻璃器具。

“你能帮我把包抬到车上去吗？”她问。我把手提箱放进车里，然后走回来帮助老太太。她扶着我的胳膊，慢慢地朝路边走去。她不停地感谢我友善的帮助。

“这没什么，”我跟她说，“我只不过用我所希望的别人对待我母亲的方式来对待我的乘客罢了。”

“哦，你是多好的一个孩子啊。”她说。我们上车后，她给了我一个地址，然后问我，“你能不能开车穿过市中心啊？”

“这可不是最近的路呀！”我很快回答说。

“哦，我不介意的，”她说，“我不赶时间。我要去趟护理所。”

我看了看后视镜，她的眼睛里闪着晶莹的光芒。

“我的家人都不在了，”她继续说，“医生说我的时间也不多了。”

我静静地伸手关掉计价器。“你想让我走哪条路线？”我问。

在接下来的两个小时里，我们开车穿越了整座城市。她带我看了她曾经做过电梯操作员的那栋大楼。我们开车经过了她和丈夫刚结婚时居住的街区。她还让我在一家家具仓库门前停车，过去那里曾是一家舞厅，当时还是个姑娘的她常常去那里跳舞。

有时，她会叫我在某栋房子或某个街角放慢车速，她坐在那里，眼睁得大大的，盯着眼前的一片漆黑，一言不发。

随着天边的太阳慢慢爬上地平线，露出最初的一丝光亮，她突然说道：“我累了，咱们走吧。”

As the first hint of sun was creasing the horizon, she suddenly said, "I'm tired. Let's go now."

We drove in silence to the address she had given me.

It was a low building, like a small **convalescent**[①] home, with a driveway that passed under a portico. Two orderlies came out to the cab as soon as we pulled up. They were solicitous and intent, watching her every move. They must have been expecting her. I opened the trunk and took the small suitcase to the door. The woman was already seated in a wheelchair.

"How much do I owe you?" she asked, reaching into her purse.

"Nothing," I said.

"You have to make a living," she answered.

"There are other passengers."

Almost without thinking, I bent and gave her a hug. She held onto me tightly.

"You gave an old woman a little moment of joy," she said. "Thank you."

I squeezed her hand, then walked into the dim morning light. Behind me, a door shut. It was the sound of the closing of a life.

I didn't pick up any more passengers that shift. I drove aimlessly, lost in thought. For the rest of that day, I could hardly talk. What if that woman had gotten an angry driver, or one who was impatient to end his shift? What if I had refused to take the run, or had honked once, then driven away?

On a quick review, I don't think that I have done anything more important in my life. We're conditioned to think that our lives revolve around great moments. But great moments often catch us unaware—beautifully wrapped in what others may consider a small one.

---

① convalescent [ˈkɔnvəˈlesnt] a. 恢复期的；渐愈的；调养的

我们朝她给我的地址开去，车内一片沉寂。

那是一座低矮的建筑，就像一座小型疗养院，有一条车道在门廊下穿过。我们刚停下车，两个疗养员就走上前来。他们殷勤又热心，细心地看着她的一举一动。他们一定是在等待她的到来。我打开后备箱，把那只小手提箱送到门边。这时，老太太已经坐在轮椅上了。

“我应该给你多少钱呢？”她问道，一边伸手到钱包里取钱。

“不用啦。”我说。

“你还得生活呀。”她回答说。

“还有其他乘客呢。”

几乎不假思索地，我弯下腰来拥抱了她。她也紧紧地抱着我。

“你给一位老人带来了片刻的欢乐，”她说，“谢谢你。”

我捏了捏她的手，然后转身走向屋外淡淡的晨曦。在我身后，传来一扇门关闭的声音，仿佛那是生命即将结束的声音。

在那趟班上，我没再载任何客人。我漫无目的地开着车，陷入了深深的沉思中。那天，我几乎很少开口说话。如果去接老太太的是一名愤怒的司机，或者是一名不耐烦的急着交班的司机，结果会怎样？如果我拒绝老人载她四处看看的要求，或者我只鸣了一次喇叭就开车离去，结果又会怎样？

我快速地回顾了一下自己的人生，我觉得这是我做过的最重要的一件事。我们习惯性地认为我们的生活总是被各种伟大的时刻所围绕着；但是，伟大的时刻常常在我们不经意间就悄然而至，并巧妙地包裹着很多人以为不足为奇的平常外衣。

Transforming Judgment Into Love

少一些评价，多一些关爱

◎ Fred Burks

I am very blessed to have come to a place where it is fairly easy for me to feel acceptance and love for almost everyone I meet. As arrogance has been the biggest challenge in myself throughout my life, the few times I find myself having difficulty accepting and loving another person now, it is usually because I see and judge in them **unbridled**① arrogance.

In this last month, I had a most amazing opportunity which challenged me to be able to accept arrogance in another and find love for him in a very profound way. George is an instructor who I interpreted for almost two years ago in a two-week course for Indonesian investigative police. George had the nasty habit of criticizing and **belittling**② almost everything everyone did in the course. He believed being harsh and critical was the best way to make the students try harder. Though the students did learn, he did a very good job of making every participant feel inferior to him by the end of the course. One woman even cried at one point as George called her everything but stupid in how she performed an exercise.

By the end of that two weeks, I couldn't wait to get away from George. I

---

① unbridled [ʌn'braidld] a. 无拘束的；激烈的；放纵的

② belittle [bi'litl] v. 轻视，贬低；使相形见小

美丽语录

Any judgment I have of others is on some level a reflection of myself.

—Fred Burks

我对他人的任何评判在某种程度上反映出自己身上的种种不足。

——弗雷德·伯克斯

很幸运地，我已经达到了一种境界，我能很容易地接受并关爱我所遇见的几乎每一个人。但是，傲慢自大是我一生中遇到的最大的挑战。现在偶尔有那么几次，我发现自己很难接受和关爱另一个人，这通常也是因为我在他们身上看到了肆无忌惮的傲慢。

就在上个月，我得到一个绝佳的机会，挑战自己去接受另一个人身上的傲慢，并深沉地去爱他。大约两年前，乔治在为期两周的印尼警方调查课程中担任讲师，当时我曾经给他做过口译。他有一个令人讨厌的习惯，他总是批评和贬低每个人在课程里做的几乎每一件事。他认为，苛刻和批评是促使学生更加努力学习的最好方法。学生们的确学到了一些东西，但他也成功地使每个学生在课程结束后都觉得自惭形秽，远不如他。一位女学生有一回甚至被弄哭了，因为乔治把她某次练习中的表现称为愚不可及。

那两个星期结束后，我迫不及待地想要离开乔治，因为我从未遇到过像他这样傲慢自大而又麻木不仁的人。那时，我很清楚我没能接受他，更

had never encountered someone so arrogant and insensitive. I was very aware at the time that I had failed to find acceptance and love for him, yet I just hoped I wouldn't have to work with him again.

Last month at another two-week training, I didn't realize until it was already too late that I would be working with George again. But I have grown a lot in the last two years, so I was able to see this training clearly as a powerful challenge and opportunity for me to try my best to accept George for who he is.

So this time, from the very first day I consciously choose to look past my judgment. I chose instead to focus on opening to the deeper part of George, to his divine light within. I chose to do my best not to try to change him, but rather to try to accept and understand him for who he is. As I opened to that deeper part of him, I was able to feel his pain and woundedness. I had a sense that somehow he had been severely criticized and belittled as a child—just as I had. I felt his deep need to compensate for this by proving both to himself and others that he was better than everyone else. This may well have led to the arrogance I saw in him, the same arrogance I dealt with so much early in my life. I realized that it was my own **righteousness**[①] about having overcome my arrogance which made me judge George so harshly. That which I had come from is what triggered me most and what I judged most severely.

With these realizations, I was for the first time able to open to seeing George for all that he is. During breaks we had a number of rich conversations about his personal life. He told me meaningful things like how much he loved being a father and how his daughter so loved him. He told me how important it was for him to be very strict with this daughter as a way of loving her.

During one lunch break, I gathered my courage and shared with him how

---

① righteousness ['raitʃəsnis] n. 正当，正义；正直

别说去爱他，我只是希望我不用再次与他共事。

上个月，又一期两周培训开始了，我发现我不得不与乔治再次共事，因为等我反应过来时已经太迟了。但是，在过去的两年里，我成长了很多，我能够把这次培训视为一次有力的挑战，也是一次难得的机会，让我能尽全力接受真实的乔治。

所以这一次，从最初的第一天起，我就有意识地选择忽略我以前的判断。我选择以开放的心态专注于更深层的乔治，专注于他的内在散发出来的神圣光芒。我选择尽量不要试图改变他，而是努力接受和理解真实的他。当我打开心扉深入他的内心时，我能够感觉到他的痛苦和创伤。我有一种预感，不知何故，他在孩提时代应该曾饱受严厉的批评和贬低，就像我小时候一样。我觉得他内心深处有一种迫切的需要，需要通过向自己和他人证明他比任何人做得都更好，来弥补小时候的心灵创伤。这很可能就导致了我在他身上看见的傲慢。在我早年的生活里，我也曾费尽心思消除我内心里与他同样的傲慢。我意识到，正是我自己成功克服傲慢所获得的正义感，促使我如此苛刻地评判乔治，这也解释了到底是什么东西触发了我，让我对他做出了最严苛的主观评判。

意识到这些以后，我第一次能够释然地面对真实的乔治。在休息时，我们聊了很多关于他个人生活的话题。他告诉了我一些很有意义的事，比如他多么喜欢做一个父亲，以及他的女儿有多么爱他。他告诉我说，他总是严格要求女儿，并以这样严格的方式爱她，这对他来说非常重要。

一次午餐时，我鼓起勇气和他谈起以前的课程对我来说多么难熬，因

difficult the previous course had been for me as I had felt he was excessively critical with the students. I told him I still felt this, but that now I wanted to get to know him and understand why he did what he did. He heard me and clearly respected my deep desire to be honest and open with me. He shared very deeply about why he acts the way he does. He even acknowledged that he is overly harsh at times. We shared in a number of deep, meaningful talks. By the end of the course, we left feeling a sincere bond of friendship and trust. I had found not only acceptance and understanding, but even a sincere love for George and for what he is trying to do.

Amazingly, throughout this course, George was significantly less critical and belittling than he had been two years earlier. He even praised people a number of times—something he had almost never done before. My own unresolved arrogance led to the thought that my openness had caused this change. Yet as soon as this thought arose, I recognized its source and quickly corrected myself. Yes, my openness and acceptance of George in these two weeks may have inspired him in some small way to be more open and less critical. Yet I also recognize that like me, he is learning and growing as he grows older, too. He is learning to be more supportive, and I am learning to be less **judgmental**① and more loving.

What a powerful lesson for me! What a wonderful change! Now, when I see people with unbridled arrogance and my judgment kicks in, I feel inspired to more easily recognize what's happening. I am inspired to look deeper to find acceptance and love of even people with a lot of arrogance, for we are all sacred creations of God. Now, I can recognize my own weakness. I can more easily recognize my own judgment which keeps me from accepting others as they are. After this empowering experience, I am inspired even more to support every

① judgmental [dʒʌdʒ'mentl] a. 判断的；审判的

为我觉得他对学生过于苛责了。我告诉他现在我仍然这么认为，但是，现在我想要了解他，理解他为什么要这么做。他听着我的话，显然非常尊重我深切的渴望，希望我们之间能开诚布公。他深刻地分享了他为什么会有这种行为方式的原因。他甚至承认，有些时候他是过于严厉了。我们共享了许多深刻、有意义的谈话。课程结束后分开时，我们都能感觉到真诚的友谊和信任。我发现自己不仅接受并理解了他，而且能真诚地去爱他以及他想做的事。

令人惊讶的是，在这次培训课程中，乔治比两年之前明显减少了批评和贬低。他甚至称赞了学生们很多次，这是他以前几乎从未做过的。我内心仍未消除的傲慢让我以为，是自己的开明导致了这种变化。然而，这个想法刚一冒出来，我就认出了它的来源，迅速纠正了我自己。是的，在这两个星期里，我的开明和接受可能以细微的方式启发了他，让他变得更开明、更乐于肯定和赞美他人。然而，我也认识到，像我一样，随着年纪的增长，他也学习和成长了。他正在学会给予他人更多的支持和帮助，而我则在学习少一些评判、多一些关爱。

对我而言，这是多么有益的一课！这是多么美妙的改变！现在，每当我看到人们肆无忌惮的傲慢，而我的主观评判便随即介入时，我就更容易觉察到这中间是怎么回事。我总是会深受启发，试图看得更深入一些，去接纳与关爱这些无比傲慢的人们，因为我们都是上帝神圣的创造。现在，我能认识到自己的弱点。我能更容易地意识到，是我的主观评判妨碍了自己去接受他人的真实面貌。有了这次赋予人力量的经历后，我深受启发，

person, arrogant or not, to be the best they can be. Thank you so much George, and thank you Spirit and my GCA friends, for helping me so beautifully to transform judgment into love.

也更加支持每个人；无论他们傲慢与否，都要帮助他们达到最好状态。非常感谢乔治，感谢神灵和我的朋友们，帮助我那么漂亮地把主观评判转变成了无私的关爱。

Chapter 3

永不放弃梦

The key is to listen to your heart and let it carry you in the direction of your dreams. And each day that you're moving toward your dreams without compromising who you are, you're winning.

—— *Michael Dell*

聆听你内心的声音，并让它带你前往梦想的方向。当你每天朝着梦想前进，而且没有放弃做自己，你就是胜利的。

——迈克尔・戴尔

Ask, Ask, Ask

请求，请求，再请求

© Jack Canfield & Mark V. Hansen

The greatest saleswoman in the world today doesn't mind if you call her a girl. That's because Markita Andrews has generated more than eighty thousand dollars selling Girl Scout cookies since she was seven years old.

Going door-to-door after school, the painfully shy Markita transformed herself into a cookie-selling **dynamo**[1] when she discovered, at age 13, the secret of selling.

It starts with desire. Burning, white-hot desire.

For Markita and her mother, who worked as a waitress in New York after her husband left them when Markita was eight years old, their dream was to travel the globe. "I'll work hard to make enough money to send you to college," her mother said one day. "You'll go to college and when you graduate, you'll make enough money to take you and me around the world. Okay?"

So at age 13 when Markita read in her Girl Scout magazine that the Scout who sold the most cookies would win an all-expenses-paid trip for two around the world, she decided to sell all the Girl Scout cookies she could—more Girl Scout cookies than anyone in the world, ever.

---

① dynamo ['dainəməu] n. 发电机；精力充沛的人

美丽语录

All your dreams can come true if you have the courage to pursue them.

—Walt Disney

你所有的梦想皆可实现，只要你有勇气去追求。

——沃尔特·迪斯尼

现今世界上最伟大的女售货员玛姬塔·安德鲁斯并不介意被称作女孩。这是因为从 7 岁至今，她已经销售了价值超过 8 万美元的童子军饼干。

放学后挨家挨户兜售，使原来极度害羞的玛姬塔变成了售卖饼干的小精灵，并在她 13 岁时发现了销售的秘诀。

这一切都始于她心中的渴望，那如火焰般燃烧的白热化的渴望。

玛姬塔的母亲曾是一名在纽约工作的女服务员，当她的丈夫离开她们时，玛姬塔只有 8 岁。玛姬塔和母亲的梦想是环球旅行。“我要努力工作赚钱，送你去上大学。”有一天，她的妈妈说。“你必须去上大学。大学毕业时，你要赚足够多的钱带咱俩周游世界。好吗？”

所以，在 13 岁时，当玛姬塔在她的女童子军杂志上读到，卖掉最多饼干的童子军将赢得双人免费游览世界各地的机会时，她决定尽其所能卖掉尽可能多的女童子军饼干——比世界上任何人卖掉的女童子军饼干都要多。

但是，光有强烈渴望是远远不够的，要实现梦想，玛姬塔知道她必须制定一个计划。

“总是注意穿着得体，你得穿上你的职业装束，”她的阿姨建议道。“当

But desire alone is not enough. To make her dream come true, Markita knew she needed a plan.

"Always wear your right outfit, your professional garb," her aunt advised. "When you are doing business, dress like you are doing business. Wear your Girl Scout uniform. When you go up to people in their **tenement**[1] buildings at 4:30 or 6:30 and especially on Friday night, ask for a big order. Always smile, whether they buy or not, always be nice. And don't ask them to buy your cookies; ask them to invest."

Lots of other Scouts may have wanted that trip around the world. Lots of other Scouts may have had a plan. But only Markita went off in her uniform each day after school, ready to ask—and keep asking—folks to invest in her dream. "Hi, I have a dream. I'm earning a trip around the world for me and my mom by merchandising Girl Scout cookies," she'd say at the door. "Would you like to invest in one dozen or two dozen boxes of cookies?"

Markita sold 3,526 boxes of Girl Scout cookies that year and won her trip around the world. Since then, she has sold more than 42,000 boxes of Girl Scout cookies, spoken at sales conventions across the country, starred in a Disney movie about her adventure and has co-authored the best seller, How to Sell More Cookies, Condos, Cadillacs, Computers...And Everything Else.

Markita is no smarter and no more extroverted than thousands of other people, young and old, with dreams of their own. The difference is Markita had discovered the secret of selling: Ask, Ask, Ask! Many people fail before they even begin because they fail to ask for what they want. The fear of rejection leads many of us to reject ourselves and our dreams long before anyone else ever has the chance—no matter what we're selling.

① tenement ['tenimənt] n. 房屋，住户，租户

你做生意时，你必须穿得像做生意的人。你必须穿上你的女童子军制服。当你在每天 4:30 或 6:30 去人们租住的公寓时，特别是在周五晚上，你可以请求人们下个大订单。你必须时刻保持微笑，对人们好些，无论他们购买与否。不要要求他们买你的饼干，要求他们向你投资。”

很多其他的童子军可能也想要环游世界。他们可能也有一个计划。但只有玛姬塔每天放学后就穿上她的制服，准备好了去请求——不停地请求人们为她的梦想投资。“你好，我有一个梦想。我想通过销售女童子军饼干为我和妈妈赢得一次环球旅行，”她会在门口说，“你愿意为我的梦想投资一打或两打饼干吗？”

那一年，玛姬塔卖出了 3,526 箱女童子军饼干，赢得了她的环球旅行。从那时起，她一共卖出了超过 42,000 箱女童子军饼干。她在全国销售会议上发表演讲，主演以她的经历为题材的迪士尼电影，与他人共同撰写了畅销书《如何卖出更多的饼干、公寓、凯迪拉克、电脑……以及其他的一切》。

与其他成千上万怀抱梦想的或年轻或年老的人们相比，玛姬塔并没有比他们更聪明或更外向。不同的是，玛姬塔发现了销售的秘诀：请求，请求，再请求！许多人甚至在开始之前就失败了，因为他们难以开口请求他们想要的东西。无论我们销售什么，对被拒绝的恐惧导致了我们中的许多人，在任何人有机会拒绝我们之前，首先否定了我们自己和我们的梦想。

然而，我们每个人都在销售。“你每天都在推销自己，在学校，向你的老板，向你刚刚认识的人，”14 岁的玛姬塔说道。“我的母亲是一位女服务员：她推销每天的特色菜。试图获得选票的市长和总统也在推销……目光所到之处，我都能看到销售。销售是整个世界的一部分。”

And everyone is selling something. "You're selling yourself everyday—in school, to your boss, to new people you meet," said Markita at 14. "My mother is a waitress: she sells the daily special. Mayors and presidents trying to get votes are selling...I see selling everywhere I look. Selling is part of the whole world."

It takes courage to ask for what you want. Courage is not the absence of fear. It's doing what it takes despite one's fear. And, as Markita has discovered, the more you ask, the easier (and more fun) it gets.

Once, on live TV, the producer decided to give Markita her toughest selling challenge. Markita was asked to sell Girl Scout cookies to another guest on the show. "Would you like to invest in one dozen or two dozen boxes of Girl Scout cookies?" she asked.

"Girl Scout cookies? I don't buy any Girl Scout cookies!" he replied. "I'm a Federal Penitentiary warden. I put 2,000 rapists, robbers, criminals, muggers and child abusers to bed every night."

Unruffled①, Markita quickly countered, "Mister, if you take some of these cookies, maybe you won't be so mean and angry and evil. And, Mister, I think it would be a good idea for you to take some of these cookies back for every one of your 2,000 prisoners, too."

Markita asked.

The warden wrote a check.

① unruffled [ˈʌnˈrʌfld] a. 平静的；镇定的，沉着的；无波浪的

你需要勇气去请求获得你想要的东西。勇气并不是没有恐惧，而是尽管有恐惧，也还是要努力去付出。而且，正如玛姬塔发现的那样，你请求得越多，你就越容易（而且越有趣地）得到它。

在一次电视直播中，节目制作人决定给玛姬塔一个最困难的销售挑战。她被要求向在场的另一个嘉宾出售童子军饼干。"你愿意投资一打或两打女童子军饼干吗？"她问。

"女童子军饼干？我不买任何童子军饼干！"他回答说。"我是一个联邦监狱狱长。我每天晚上要安排 2,000 名犯了强奸、盗窃、抢劫、虐待儿童等罪行的囚犯上床睡觉。"

玛姬塔面不改色，很快反驳道："先生，如果你买走其中的一些饼干，也许你就不会这么刻薄、愤怒、充满邪恶了。而且，先生，我认为这是一个好主意：你把一些饼干带回去，然后送给你那 2,000 名囚犯中的每一个人。"

玛姬塔请求道。

监狱长现场就开了支票。

Paul's Unstoppable Will Power Turns Wasteland to Forest

意志的魔力

◎ Adam Khan

When Paul was a boy growing up in Utah, he happened to live near an old copper smelter. The sulfur dioxide that poured out of the refinery had made a **desolate**[①] wasteland out of what used to be a beautiful forest. When a young visitor one day looked at this wasteland and saw that there was nothing living there—no animals, no trees, no grass, no bushes, no birds...nothing but fourteen thousand acres of black and barren land that even smelled bad—well, this kid looked at the land and said, "This place is crummy." Little Paul knocked him down. He felt insulted. But he looked around him and something happened inside him. He made a decision: Paul Rokich vowed that some day he would bring back the life to this land.

Years later Paul was in the area, and he went to the smelter office. He asked if they had any plans to bring the trees back. The answer was "No." He asked if they would let him try to bring the trees back. Again, the answer was "No." They didn't want him on their land. He realized he needed to be more knowledgeable before anyone would listen to him, so he went to college to study botany.

At the college he met a professor who was an expert in Utah's ecology.

---

① desolate ['desəleit,'desəlit] a. 荒凉的，荒芜的，孤单寂寞的

美丽语录

The difference in winning and losing is most often... not quitting.

—Walt Disney

赢与输的差别通常是……不放弃。

——沃尔特·迪斯尼

保罗在犹他州长大，那时他碰巧住在一个老旧的铜冶炼厂里。冶炼厂排出的二氧化硫，使这里曾经美丽的森林已经变成一片荒凉的废墟。有一天，一位年轻游客看着这片荒芜的土地，这片满目疮痍——没有动物，没有草木，没有灌木丛，没有鸟……除了一万四千英亩散发着恶臭的贫瘠的黑色土地，他望着土地，说："这个地方实在是糟糕透顶。"小保罗把他打倒在地，因为他感觉受到了侮辱。但是，当保罗朝四周看了看后，内心发生了细微的变化。他做出了一个决定：保罗·洛基希发誓，总有一天，他会把生机和活力带回这片土地上。

几年后，保罗回到了该地区，去了冶炼厂的办公室。他问他们是否有计划把树重新种起来。答案是"没有"。他问他们是否可以让他重新把树种起来。又一次得到答案："不行。"他们不想让他留在他们的土地上。他意识到，在有人听从他的建议之前，他需要更多的知识，所以他开始去大学学习植物学。

在大学里，保罗遇到了一位教授，他是犹他州生态学专家。不幸的是，

Unfortunately, this expert told Paul that the wasteland he wanted to bring back was beyond hope. He was told that his goal was foolish because even if he planted trees, and even if they grew, the wind would only blow the seeds forty feet per year, and that's all you'd get because there weren't any birds or squirrels to spread the seeds, and the seeds from those trees would need another thirty years before they started producing seeds of their own. Therefore, it would take approximately twenty thousand years to **revegetate**① that six-square-mile piece of earth.

So he tried to go on with his life. He got a job operating heavy equipment, got married, and had some kids. But his dream would not die. He kept studying up on the subject, and he kept thinking about it. And then one night, Paul looked at what opportunities were right in front of him. He decided to get up and take some action. He would do what he could with what he had. This was an important turning point.

Under the cover of darkness, he sneaked out into the wasteland with a backpack full of seedlings and started planting. For seven hours he planted seedlings. He did it again a week later. And every week, he made his secret journey into the wasteland and planted trees and shrubs and grass. But most of it died. For fifteen years he did this. When a whole valley of his fir seedlings burned to the ground because of a careless sheepherder, Paul broke down and wept. Then he got up and kept planting.

Freezing winds and **blistering**② heat, landslides and floods and fires destroyed his work time and time again. But he kept planting. One night he found a highway crew had come and taken tons of dirt for a road grade, and all

---

① revegetate [ri:'vedʒiteit] v. [植] 再生长，再植

② blistering ['blistəriŋ] a. 快的；酷热的；起泡的；激烈的

这种专家告诉保罗，他不可能复原荒地。他被告知他的目标是愚蠢的，因为即使他种植了树木，即使树木会成长，大风也只会以每年 40 英尺的速度把种子散播开去，这就是你能得到的全部自然力量；因为没有任何鸟类或松鼠传播种子，这些树木产生的种子将需要再过 30 年才能开始产生自己的种子。因此，大约需要 2 万年时间才能使 6 平方英里的土地重新披上绿色植被。

于是，他试图继续过着自己的生活。他得到了一份操作重型设备的工作，结婚生子，有了几个孩子。但他并没有放弃梦想。他一直钻研着这个课题，不停地思考它。此后的一天晚上，保罗仔细想了想摆在他面前的机会有哪些。他决定起床采取一些行动。他将倾其所有、尽其所能去做些事情。这是一个重要的转折点。

在夜幕的掩护下，他背着装满树苗的背包，偷偷溜回荒地，开始种起树来。他栽了整整 7 个小时的树苗。一个星期后，他又种了一次。此后的每一周，他都会隐秘地回到荒地，种植树木、灌木、草皮。但是，大部分都活不下来。连续 15 年间，他一直坚持这样做。一次，因为牧羊人的粗心大意，整个山谷的杉木苗一度被烧殆尽，保罗忍不住失声痛哭。然而，之后他又站了起来，继续种树。

刺骨的寒风，炙烤般的酷热，山体滑坡，洪水，火灾，这些一次又一次摧毁了他的杰作。但他坚持一直种下去。有一天晚上，他发现来了一队高速公路养护员，他们从地里挖取了数吨泥土来填实道路斜坡，而他煞费

the plants he had painstakingly planted in that area were gone. But he just kept planting.

Week after week, year after year he kept at it, against the opinion of the authorities, against the trespassing laws, against the devastation of road crews, against the wind and rain and heat...even against plain common sense. He just kept planting. Slowly, very slowly, things began to take root. Then gophers appeared. Then rabbits. Then porcupines.

Eventually, the old copper smelter saw the results and gave him permission to plant. Then later, as times were changing and there was political pressure to clean up the environment, the company actually hired Paul to do what he was already doing, and they provided him with machinery and crews to work with. Progress accelerated. Now the place is fourteen thousand acres of trees and grass and bushes, rich with elk and eagles, and Paul Rokich has received almost every environmental award Utah has.

Recently, Paul mused on his long decades of dedicated work, "I thought that if I got this started, when I was dead and gone people would come and see it. I never thought I'd live to see it myself!" It took him until his hair turned white, but he managed to keep that impossible vow he made to himself as a child.

What was it you wanted to do that you thought was impossible? Paul's story sure gives a **perspective** ④ [①] on things, doesn't it? The way you get something accomplished in this world is to just keep planting. Just keep working. Just keep plugging away at it one day at a time for a long time, no matter who criticizes you, no matter how long it takes, no matter how many times you fall. Get back up again. And just keep planting.

---

① perspective [pə'spektiv] n. 远景；看法；透视

苦心种植在那个地区的所有植物都被他们铲除了。但他还是继续种着。

一周又一周，一年复一年，他一直坚持种着，不顾当地政府的意见，不顾擅自进入行为的法律约束，不顾捣蛋破坏的公路养护队，顶着狂风暴雨酷暑严寒……甚至不顾最简单不过的常识。他就一直种着。慢慢地，很慢很慢地，事情有了转机；植物开始生根，地鼠出现了，然后兔子出现了，再然后豪猪也出现了。

最终，老铜矿冶炼厂看到了他努力的结果，并允许他种植。后来，随着时代的变化，清理环境的政治压力不断增大，公司实际上雇佣了保罗做他一直在做的事情，他们给他提供了机械和工作人员一起工作。进展不断加速。现在这一万四千英亩的土地上方种满了树木、灌木和青草，到处都可见麋鹿和老鹰，而保罗已经获得了犹他州几乎每一个环境奖项。

最近，保罗回想起几十年如一日努力忘我的工作时说："我想，如果我开始做这件事情，当我死了以后，人们会来看看它。我从未想过自己能活着亲眼见证这一切！"为了实现孩提时代对自己许下的看似不可能的誓言，他几乎花了一辈子的时间，直到他成了头发花白的老人。

什么事情是你想做却又认为是不可能的？保罗的故事的确可以给这些事情提供一个视角，不是吗？在这个世界上，你要取得一些成就的秘诀就是，继续坚持。你只要继续坚持工作，每天坚持做一点并坚持很长时间，不管谁批评你，无论需要多长时间，不管你跌倒多少次，都记得再次站起来，然后继续坚持下去。

Finding My Wings

展开梦想的翅膀

◎ Sue Augustine

Reach high, for stars lie hidden in your soul. Dream deep, for every dream precedes the goal.

—Pamela Vaull Starr

Like so many other girls, my self-confidence growing up was almost nonexistent. I doubted my abilities, had little faith in my potential and questioned my personal worth. If I achieved good grades, I believed that I was just lucky. Although I made friends easily, I worried once they got to know me, the friendships wouldn't last. And when things went well, I thought I was just in the right place at the right time. I even rejected praise and compliments.

The choice I made reflected my self-image. While in my teens, I attracted a man with the same low self-esteem. In spite of his violent temper and an extremely rocky dating relationship, I decided to marry him. I still remember my dad whispering to me before walking me down the **aisle**[1], "It's not too late, Sue. You can change your mind." My family knew what a terrible mistake I was making. Within weeks, I knew it, too.

① aisle [ail] n. 侧廊，（席位间的）通道

美丽语录

You cannot control what happens to you, but you can control your attitude toward what happens to you, and in that, you will be mastering change rather than allowing it to master you.

—Brian Tracy

你不能控制发生在你身上的事，但你可以控制看待它的态度。而这么做时，你将可以掌控改变，而不是让改变掌控你。

——布莱恩·崔西

跳得更高，因为你内心深藏着对天际星辰的渴望；梦得更深，因为每一个梦想都让你不断靠近最终的理想。

——帕梅拉·维奥尔·斯塔尔

像很多女孩一样，我的自信心几乎从未成长过。我怀疑自己的能力，不相信自己有潜力，质疑自己的个人价值。如果我取得了好成绩，我认为那只不过是运气罢了。虽然我很容易交到朋友，但我担心一旦他们了解了我，友谊便不会持久。当事情进展十分顺利时，我认为那只不过是合适的时间、地点作用的结果。我甚至拒绝表扬和赞美。

我所做的选择反映了我的自我形象。在我十几岁时，我吸引了一名自尊心和我同样脆弱的男人。尽管他脾气暴躁，我们恋爱时的关系极度起伏，并不美满，但我仍然决定要嫁给他。我依然记得爸爸在陪我走向婚姻圣坛之前时，向我低声耳语道："现在改变你的想法，还不算太晚，苏。"我的家人知道我正在犯一个可怕的错误。几周之后，我自己也明白了。

家庭暴力持续了好几年。我遭受了严重的伤害，大部分时间我的身体

The physical abuse lasted for several years. I survived serious injures, was covered with bruises much of the time and had to be hospitalized on numerous occasions. Life became a blur of police **sirens**[①], doctor's reports and family court appearances. Yet I continued to go back to the relationship, hoping that things would somehow improve.

After we had our two little girls, there were times when all that got me through the night was having those chubby little arms wrapped around my neck, pudgy cheeks pressed up against mine and precious toddler voices saying, "It's all right, Mummy. Everything will be okay."But I knew that it wasn't going to be okay. I had to make changes—if not for myself, to protect my little girls.

Then something gave me the courage to change. Through work, I was able to attend a series of professional development seminars. In one, a presenter talked about turning dreams into realities. That was hard for me—even to dream about a better future. But something in the message made me listen.

She asked us to consider two powerful questions: "If you could be, do, or have anything in the world, and you knew it would be impossible to fail, what would you choose? And if you could create your ideal life, what would you dare to dream?" In that moment, my life began to change. I began to dream.

I imagined having the courage to move the children into an apartment of our own and start over. I pictured a life for the girls and me. I dreamed about being an international motivational speaker so that I could inspire people the way the seminar leader had inspired me. I saw myself writing my story to encourage others.

So I went on to create a visual picture of my new success. I envisioned myself wearing a business suit, carrying a leather briefcase and getting on an

① siren ['saiərin] n. 汽笛；警报器

都遍布瘀伤，无数次我不得不入院治疗。生活开始成为充斥着模糊的警笛声、医生报告、出席家庭法庭的可怕噩梦。然而，每一次我总会回到我们的婚姻中去，希望事情会有所好转。

后来，我们有了两个小女孩。孩子们的陪伴让我熬过了一个又一个漫漫长夜。她们胖乎乎的手臂环抱着我的脖子，胖乎乎的脸颊挤压着我的脸，用学步孩童娇滴滴的声音说："没关系，妈妈。一切都会好的。"但我知道事情不会好了。我不得不做出改变——即使不是为了我自己，也是为了保护我年幼的女儿们。

后来，我逐渐能拿出勇气去尝试改变。因为工作的关系，我参加了一系列职业发展研讨会。在一次会上，一位演讲者谈论的话题是如何把梦想变为现实。那对我来说非常困难——我甚至很难去想象更好的未来。但是，其中的一些信息吸引了我驻足倾听。

她让我们考虑两个重大的问题："如果你可以在这世界上成为什么，做什么，或者拥有什么，而且你不会失败，你会选择什么？如果你可以创造属于自己的理想生活，你敢于梦想吗？"在那一刻，我的生活开始发生变化，我开始了梦想。

我想象着我有足够的勇气带着孩子住进自己的公寓，一切都重新开始。我想象着我和孩子们的生活。我梦想成为一名国际励志演说家，这样我就可以激发他人，就像研讨会的演讲者启发了我那样。我似乎已经看到自己把亲身经历写下来，并以此鼓励其他人。

所以，我继续在脑海里想象我取得新的成功时的情景。我想象自己穿着西装，带着一个皮革公文包，登上一架飞机。对于我而言，那是一个相当大的跨越，因为当时的我甚至穷得都买不起西装。

airplane. This was quite a **stretch**① for me, since at the time I couldn't even afford a suit.

Yet I knew that if I was going to dream, it was important to fill in the details for my five senses. So I went to the leather store and modeled a briefcase in front of the mirror. How would it look and feel? What does leather smell like? I tried on some red suits and even found a picture of a woman in a red suit, carrying a briefcase and getting on a plane. I hung the picture up where I could see it every day. It helped me to keep the dream alive.

And soon the changes began. I moved with the children to a small apartment. On only $98 a week, we ate a lot of peanut butter and drove an old car. But for the first time, we felt free and safe. I worked hard at my sales career, all the time focusing on my "impossible dream".

Then one day I answered the phone, and the voice on the other end asked me to speak at the company's upcoming annual conference. I accepted, and my speech was a success. This led to a series of promotions, eventually to a national trainer. I went on to develop my own speaking company and have traveled to many countries around the world. My impossible dream has become a reality.

I believe that all success begins with spreading your wings—believing in your worth, trusting in your insight, nurturing yourself, having a goal and devising a personal **strategy**②. And then, even impossible dreams become real.

---

① stretch [stretʃ] n. 伸展；张开；弹性

② strategy ['strætidʒi] n. 策略，战略

但我知道，如果我要梦想，为我的五种感官填补细节信息就非常重要。所以我去了皮革商店，在镜子前看着自己提着公文包的样子。它看起来怎样，摸起来感觉如何？闻上去怎样？我试穿了几件红色套装，甚至看见那里真有一张穿红色套装的女人带着公文包乘坐飞机的照片。我把照片挂在每天都能看到的地方，它帮我保持梦想，让它始终都生动鲜活。

很快，生活开始发生变化了。我和孩子们搬进了一套小公寓。我们每周只有 98 美元用于生活开支，我们吃很多的花生酱，开一辆旧汽车。但是有史以来第一次，我们感到自由和安全。我努力做我的销售工作，把所有的时间都专注于我那“不可能实现的梦想”。

有一天，我接到了一个电话，对方邀请我在公司即将推出的年度会议上发表演讲。我接受了，而且我的演讲获得了成功。这引发了一系列的宣传活动，最终，我成为一位国内知名的培训讲师。我继续发展自己的演讲事业，并前往世界各地的许多国家进行演讲培训。我不可能实现的梦想已成为现实。

我相信，所有的成功都来源于展开梦想的翅膀——相信你的价值，相信你的洞察力，培养自己，制定目标和个人策略。最后，不可能实现的梦想甚至也能成为现实。

His Life's Work
一辈子的工作

◎ Wyverne Flatt

When his wife died, the baby was two. The six other children—three boys and three girls, range in age from 4 to 16.

A few days after he became a widower, the man's parents and his wife's parents came to visit.

"We've been talking," they said, "about how to make this work. There's no way you can take care of all these children and make a living. So, we've arranged for each child and be placed with a different uncle and aunt. We're making sure that all of your children will be living right here in the neighborhood, so you can see them anytime..."

"You have no diea how much I appreciate your thoughtfulness," the man said. "But I want you to know," he smiled and continued, "if the children should interfere with my work, or if we should need any help, we'll let you know."

Over the next few weeks the man worked with his children, assigning them chores and giving them responsibilities. The two older girls, aged 12 and 10, began to cook and do the laundry and household chores. The two older boys, 16 and 14, helped their father with farming.

But then another blow came. The man developed **arthritis**[①]. His hands

① arthritis [ɑː'θraitis] n. 关节炎

美丽语录

A man does what he must—in spite of personal consequences, in spite of obstacles and dangers and pressures.

—John Kennedy

一个人要有所担当——不在乎个人后果，不在乎困难、危险及压力。

——约翰·肯尼迪

他妻子去世的时候，最小的孩子刚满两岁，其他六个孩子，三男三女，最小的才 4 岁，最大的也就 16 岁。

他成为鳏夫后，过了几天，他的父母和岳父母双双来到他家里。

“我们已经讨论过以后该怎么办了。”他们说，“你不可能一边照顾所有的孩子，一边工作谋得生计。所以，我们把每个孩子安排到各个叔叔阿姨家里去。我们保证所有的孩子都会生活在附近，你可以在任何时候见到他们……”

“你们不知道我有多么感激你们的体贴周到，”男人说，“但我想让你们知道，”他笑了笑，接着说，“如果孩子们影响了我的工作，或者我们需要任何帮助，我会通知你们的。”

在接下来的几个星期里，男人与他的孩子们一起干活；他给他们分配杂活儿，让他们担当责任。两个年长的女孩，分别是 12 岁和 10 岁，开始做饭、洗衣服，料理家务；两个年长的男孩，分别是 16 岁和 14 岁，帮助他们的父亲干些农活。

但是紧接着，他们遭到了另一个打击——男人患了关节炎。他的手高

swelled, and he was unable to use his farm tools. The children shouldered their loads well, but the man could see that he would not be able to continue in this way. He sold his farming equipment, moved the family to a small town and opened a small business.

The family was welcomed into the new neighbourhood. The man's business **flourished**[①]. He **derived**[②] pleasure from seeing people and serving them. Word of his pleasant personality and excellent customer service began to spread. People came from far and wide to do business with him. And the children helped both at home and at work. Their father's pleasure in his work brought satisfaction to them, and he drew pleasure from their successes.

The children grew up and got married. Five of the seven went off to college, most after they were married. Each one paid his or her own way. The children's collegiate successes were a source of pride to the father. He had stopped at the sixth grade.

Then came grandchildren. No one enjoyed grandchildren more than this man. As they became toddlers, he invited them to his workplace and his small home. They brought each other great joy.

Finally, the youngest daughter—the baby who had been two years old at her mother's death—got married.

And the man, his life's work completed, died.

This man's work had been the lonely but joyful task of raising his family. This man was my father. I was the 16-year-old, the oldest of seven.

① flourish ['flʌriʃ] v. 茂盛，繁荣；挥舞；活跃

② derive [di'raiv] v. 获取；得自；起源

高肿了起来，无法使用农具了。孩子们挑起了家庭的重担，但是男人明白，他无法这样继续下去。他卖掉了农业设备，全家搬到了一个小镇上，开始经营起小生意。

这个家庭在小镇上受到了人们的欢迎。男人的生意也很红火。他接待人们，为他们提供服务，并从中得到了快乐。他开朗和善的性格，以及给客户提供的优良服务，在人们之间口口相传。人们从四面八方赶来与他做生意。孩子们在家庭事务和生意上都提供了极大的帮助。父亲在生意上获得的喜悦让孩子们感到满足，而他也为孩子们的成功感到十分愉悦。

孩子们长大了，结婚了。七个孩子中的五个上了大学，大多数是婚后上的大学，每个人都自己负责上大学的费用。孩子们在大学获得的成功让他们的父亲引以为豪。而他自己只上了六年级就辍学了。

后来，孙子孙女也出生了。没有人比他更喜欢孙子孙女了。当他们蹒跚学步之时，他把他们带到工作的地方和他的小房子里。他们给彼此带来了巨大的乐趣。

最后，最小的女儿——母亲去世时才 2 岁的婴儿——也结婚了。

这个男人，他一辈子的工作终于完成了。他去世了。

男人一直孤独但却快乐地养育着他的家人，这是他一辈子的工作。这个男人是我的父亲，而我就是那个 16 岁的男孩，七个孩子中最年长的那个。

Become What You Want to Be

奥运冠军之路

◎ Brian Cavanaugh

Let me tell you about a little girl who was born into a very poor family in a **shack**[①] in the Backwoods of Tennessee. She was the 20th of 22 children, prematurely born and frail. Her survival was doubtful. When she was four years old she had double **pneumonia**[②] and scarlet fever—a deadly combination that left her with a paralyzed and useless left leg. She had to wear an iron leg brace. Yet she was fortunate in having a mother who encouraged her.

Well, this mother told her little girl, who was very bright, that despite the brace and leg, she could do whatever she wanted to do with her life. She told her that all she needed to do was to have faith, **persistence**[③], courage and and indomitable spirit.

So at nine years of age, the little girl removed the leg brace, and she took the step the doctors told her she would never take normally. In four years, she developed a rhytmic stride, which was a medical wonder. Then this girl got the notion, the incredible notion, that she would like to be the world's greatest

---

① shack [ʃæk] n. 棚房；窝棚；小室

② pneumonia [nju:'məunjə] n. 肺炎

③ persistence [pə'sistəns] n. 坚持，毅力

美丽语录

Never underestimate the power of dreams and the influence of the human spirit. We are all the same in this notion: The potential for greatness lives within each of us.

—Wilma Rudolph

绝不要低估梦想的力量及人类心灵的作用。在这点上我们并无区别：成就伟大的潜力活在我们每个人心里。

——威尔玛·鲁道夫

让我告诉你一个小女孩的故事。她出生于田纳西州偏远棚户区一个非常贫困的家庭，在这个家庭的22个孩子中排行20。她是个虚弱的早产儿，幸存下来的几率很小。4岁的时候，她得了双侧肺炎和猩红热——一个致命的疾病组合，这场疾病使她的左腿瘫痪，她不得不用铁质支架支撑身体。然而，幸运的是，她的母亲一直鼓励着她。

这个母亲告诉她的小女孩，她非常聪明，尽管她的腿瘫痪了而必须依赖支架，但她可以按她理想的方式去生活。她告诉她，她需要的只是信心、毅力、勇气和不屈不挠的精神。

所以，9岁那年，小女孩卸下了支架。尽管医生说她永远都不能正常迈步走路，但她仍然开始练习起走路。在四年时间里，她新创了一种节奏步伐。这是一个医学奇迹。后来，这个女孩有了一个令人难以置信的想法：她想成为世界上最伟大的女子跑步运动员。那么，她是什么意思呢——成

woman runner. Now, what could she mean—be a runner with a leg like that?

At age 13, she entered a race. She came in last-way, way last. She entered every race in high school, and in every race she came in last. Everyone begged her quit! However, one day, she came in next to last. And then there came a day when she won a race. From then on, Wilma Rudolph won every race that she entered.

Wilma went to Tennessee State University, where she met a coach named Ed Temple. Coach Temple saw the indomitable spirit of the girl, that she was a believer and that she had great natural talent. He trained her so well that she went to the Olympic Games.

There she was **pitted**① against the greatest woman runner of the day, a German girl named Jutta Heine. Nobody had ever beaten Jutta. But in the 100-meter dash, Wilma Rudolph won. She beat Jutta again in the 200-meters. Now Wilma had two Olimpic gold medals.

Finally came the 400-meter relay. It would be Wilma against Jutta once again. The first two runners on Wilma's team made perfect handoffs with the baton. But when the third runner handed the baton to Wilma, she was so excited she dropped it, and Wilma saw Jutta taking off down the track. It was impossible that anybody could catch this fleet and nimble girl. But Wilma did just that! Wilma Rudolph had earned three Olympic gold medals.

① pit [pit] v. 使凹陷；使竞争

为一个有那样一条腿的跑步者?

13 岁时，她参加了一个比赛。她跑了最后一名，远远落后于其他人的真正的最后一名。她参加高中里的每一场比赛，在每场比赛中总是最后一名。每个人都恳求她退出比赛！然而，后来有一天，她跑了倒数第二名。再有一天，她居然赢得了比赛。从那时起，威尔玛·鲁道夫赢得了她所参加的每一场比赛。

威尔玛上了田纳西州立大学，在那里遇到了一位名叫艾德·坦贝尔的教练。教练在女孩身上看到了不屈不挠的精神，也看出她很有天赋，对自己很有信心。在他的训练下，女孩变得十分优秀，进而去参加了奥运会。

在奥运会上，她与当时最优秀的女运动员德国女孩尤塔·海涅同场竞技。没有人曾击败过尤塔。但在 100 米短跑中，威尔玛·鲁道夫获胜了。在 200 米中，她再次击败尤塔。现在，威尔玛有两枚奥运会金牌。

最后是 400 米接力比赛。这将是威尔玛与尤塔的再一次对决。威尔玛团队的前两名运动员完美地完成了接棒，但是当第三名运动员将接力棒传给威尔玛时，她是如此激动，以至于把它掉在了地上。威尔玛看见尤塔沿着跑道飞一般地跑去。任何人都不可能追上这个身手敏捷、健步如飞的女孩。但威尔玛却做到了！威尔玛·鲁道夫赢得了她的第三枚奥运会金牌。

I Can Make It Happen

我能做到

© Anonymous

History **abounds**[①] with tales of experts who were convinced that the ideas, plans, and projects of others could never be achieved. However, accomplishment came to those who said, "I can make it happen."

The Italian sculptor Agostino d'Antonio worked **diligently**[②] on a large piece of marble. Unable to produce his desired masterpiece, he lamented, "I can do nothing with it." Other sculptors also worked this difficult piece of marble, but to no avail. Michelangelo discovered the stone and **visualized**[③] the possibilities in it. His "I-can-make-it-happen" attitude resulted in one of the world's masterpieces—David.

The experts of Spain concluded that Columbus's plans to discover a new and shorter route to the West Indies was virtually impossible. Queen Isabella and King Ferdinand ignored the report of the experts. "I can make it happen," Columbus persisted. And he did. Everyone knew the world was flat, but not Columbus. The Nina, the Pinta, the Santa Maria, along with Columbus and his

---

① abound [ə'baund] v. 富于；充满

② diligently ['dilidʒəntli] ad. 勤奋地

③ visualize ['viʒuəlaiz] v. 使……看得见；形象化；设想

美丽语录

To accomplish great things, we must not only act, but also dream, not only plan, but also believe.

—Anatole France

为成就大事，我们需要的不只是行动，还要梦想；不只是计划，还要相信。

——阿纳托尔·法郎士

历史上流传着很多所谓“行家”或“专家”的故事，他们深信他人的某些创意、计划或项目或许永远都不能实现。但是，那些坚持认为“我能做到”的人往往并不信这个邪，并且最终取得了成功。

意大利雕刻家阿戈斯蒂诺·安东尼奥对着一大块大理石苦思冥想。他无法用它雕刻出理想的杰作，于是哀叹道：“我用它创作不出什么。”其他雕塑家也曾试图雕刻这块难以处理的大理石，但也都一无所获。米开朗基罗发现了这块石头，并在想象中呈现出它被雕刻成作品的各种可能性。他的这种“我能做到”的态度，给后世留下了闻名世界的杰作——大卫。

西班牙的专家们认为，哥伦布开发一条通往西印度群岛的较短的新路线计划几乎是不可能的。伊莎贝拉女王和费迪南国王并没有理睬这些专家

small band of followers, sailed to "impossible" new lands and thriving resources.

Even the great Thomas Alva Edison discouraged his friend, Henry Ford, from pursuing his **fledgling**[①] idea of a motorcar. Convinced of the worthlessness of the idea, Edison invited Ford to come and work for him. Ford remained committed and tirelessly pursued his dream. Although his first attempt resulted in a vehicle without reverse gear, Henry Ford knew he could make it happen. And, of course, he did.

"Forget it," the experts advised Madame Curie. They agreed radium was a scientifically impossible idea. However, Marie Curie insisted, "I can make it happen."

Let's not forget our friends Orville and Wilbur Wright. Journalists, friends, armed forces specialists, and even their father laughed at the idea of an airplane. "What a silly and insane way to spend money. Leave flying to the birds," they jeered. "Sorry," the Wright brothers responded. "We have a dream, and we can make it happen." As a result, a place called Kitty Hawk, North Carolina, became the setting for the launching of their "ridiculous" idea.

Finally, as you read these accounts under the magnificent lighting of your environment, consider the plight of Benjamin Franklin. He was admonished to stop the foolish experimenting with lighting. What an **absurdity**[②] and waste of time! Why, nothing could outdo the fabulous oil lamp. Thank goodness Franklin knew he could make it happen. You too can make it happen!

① fledgling ['fledʒliŋ] a. 刚开始的；无经验的

② absurdity [əb'sə:diti] n. 荒谬，悖理；荒谬的事

的报告。哥伦布坚持认为："我可以实现这个计划。"他做到了。每个人都认为世界是平的，但哥伦布不这么看。尼娜号、宾塔号、圣玛丽亚号，连同哥伦布和他的小规模追随者，航行到专家们所谓"不可能"的新大陆，发现了极其丰富的自然资源。

即使最伟大的发明家托马斯·阿尔瓦·爱迪生，也曾劝阻过他的朋友亨利·福特不要去投资刚刚起步的汽车行业。爱迪生相信福特的想法毫无价值，并邀请福特来为他工作。但福特仍不知疲倦地致力于追求他的梦想。尽管他的第一次尝试以失败而告终——他所生产的第一辆车居然没有反向齿轮，但亨利·福特知道他可以实现自己的梦想。而且，最后，他确实成功了。

"算了吧！"专家向居里夫人建议道。他们一致认为镭在科学上是不可能的。然而，居里夫人坚持说："我能做到。"

我们不要忘记，我们的朋友莱特兄弟，奥维尔·莱特和威尔伯·莱特。记者、朋友、军队专家、甚至他们的父亲都嘲笑他们建造一架飞机的想法。"这不过是个愚蠢而疯狂的挥霍钱财的把戏。把飞行那事儿留给天上的鸟儿吧！"他们嘲笑道。"对不起，"莱特兄弟回答，"我们有一个梦想，我们能做到。"结果，在北卡罗莱纳州一个叫基蒂霍克的地方，他们实践了在别人看来荒谬无比的想法。

最后，当你在明亮的灯光下阅读这些故事的时候，想一想本杰明·富兰克林的困境吧。他被人们屡次告诫停止愚蠢的照明试验。在当时的人们看来，那是多么荒谬而又浪费时间的试验啊！没有什么可以超越美轮美奂的油灯。幸亏，富兰克林知道他可以实现自己的梦想。别忘了，你也可以梦想成真！

Sparky
斯巴克：一个失败者的故事

◎ Brian Cavanaugh

A story is told about a boy named Sparky. For Sparky school was all but impossible. He failed every subject in the eighth grade. He **flunked**[1] physics in high school. Receiving a flat zero in the course, he distinguished himeself as the worst physics student in the school's history. Sparky also flunked Latin, algebra and English. He didn't do much better in sports. Although he did manage to make the school's golf team, he promptly lost the only important match of the season. There was a **consolation**[2] match; he lost that, too.

Throughout his youth Sparky was awkward socially. He was not actually disliked by the other students; no one cared that much. He was astonished if a classmate ever said hello to him outside of school hours. There's no way to tell how he might have done at dating. Sparky never once asked a girl to go out in high school. He was too afraid of being turned down.

Sparky was a loser. He, his classmates...everyone knew it. So he rolled with it. Sparky had made up his mind early in life that if things were meant to work out, they would. Otherwise he would content himself with what appeared to be

① flunked [flʌŋk] v.（使）失败；（使）考试不及格

② consolation [ˌkɔnsəˈleiʃən] n. 安慰，慰藉

美丽语录

Defeat is not the worst of failures. Not to have tried is the true failure.

—George Woodberry

被击倒不是最大的失败，不曾尝试才是真正的失败。

——乔治·伍德贝利

这是一个关于男孩斯巴克的故事。斯巴克在学业上的表现非常糟糕：八年级时，他每门功课都不及格；上高中时，物理不及格。他在物理课上得了个零分，成了学校历史上物理成绩最差的学生。他的拉丁语、代数、英语等课程也纷纷挂了科，连体育课成绩都不好。尽管他设法加入了学校的高尔夫球队，但他很快就在那个赛季唯一重要的比赛中落败了。在另一场安慰赛上，他也输掉了。

在斯巴克的整个青年时期，他在社交生活中总是处于尴尬的境地。实际上，其他学生并不是那么讨厌他；只是没有人在乎他。一个同学在校外时间跟他打声招呼，他都会感到非常吃惊，更别说他在约会方面会有什么上佳表现了。上高中时，他从未邀请过女孩出去约会，因为他太害怕被拒绝了。

斯巴克是一个失败者。他和他的同学们……每个人都知道这一点。所以他也习以为常了。在很早的时候，他就已经下定决心，如果一切注定会好，那么迟早会好起来的。否则，他将愉快地接受自己看起来命中注定的

his inevitable **mediocrity**①.

However, one thing was important to Sparky—drawing. He was proud of his artwork. Of course, no one else appreciated it. In his senior year of high school, he submitted some cartoons to the editors of the yearbook. They were turned down. Despite this particularly painful rejection, Sparky was so convinced of his ability that he decided to become a professional artist.

Upon graduating from high school, he wrote a letter to Walt Disney Studios. He was told to send some samples of his artwork, and the subject matter for cartoons was suggested. Sparky drew the proposed cartoon. He spent a great deal of time on it and on all the other drawings he submitted. Finally the reply came from Disney Studios, he had been rejected once again. Another loss for the loser.

So Sparky decided to write his own autobiography in cartoons. He described his childhood self—a little boy loser and **chronic**② underachiever. The cartoon character would soon become famous worldwide. For Sparky, the boy who had failed every subject in the eight grade and whose work was rejected again and again, was Charles Schulz. He created the "Peanuts" comic strip and the little cartoons boy whose kite would never fly and who never succeeded in kicking the football—Charlie Brown.

① mediocrity [ˌmiːdiˈɔkriti] n. 平常；平庸之才

② chronic [ˈkrɔnik] a. 长期的；慢性的；惯常的

平庸。

然而，有一件事对斯巴克而言非常重要——绘画。他对自己的画作引以为豪。当然，没有人会欣赏他的作品。在他上高中高年级的时候，他提交了一些卡通图画给年鉴编辑。但它们遭到了拒绝。尽管被拒绝特别痛苦，但斯巴克非常确信自己的能力，他决心成为一个职业画家。

高中毕业后，他写了一封信给迪斯尼工作室。对方要求他发些自己的卡通作品做为样本，而且，卡通的主题得是由对方提议的。斯巴克按照对方的主题画好了卡通作品。在这些作品以及他提交的其他所有绘画上，他花去了大量的时间。最后，迪斯尼工作室回复了他，他再一次被拒绝。失败者的又一个失败。

后来，斯巴克决定以卡通片的形式来撰写他的自传。他描述了童年时代的自己——一个失败的小男孩，一个学习落后的差生专业户。这个卡通人物很快闻名世界。斯巴克，那个八年级时每一门课都不及格的男孩，那个作品一次又一次被拒绝的男孩，实际上就是查尔斯·舒尔茨。他创造了“花生”系列卡通漫画，还有那个风筝永远飞不起来、从来没能成功踢足球的卡通小男孩——查理·布朗。

When Dreams Won't Die

梦想永不灭

© Marilyn Johnson Kondwani

Ever since I can remember, I've been **fascinated**[①] by beauty. As a young girl surrounded by the numbing sameness of all those cornfields around Indianapolis, the glamorous worlds of fashion and cosmetics were a magnificent escape for me. Every time I looked at the advertisements in women's magazines—all those gorgeous models with flawless skin and expertly applied makeup, their statuesque bodies adorned with **incredible**[②] designer outfits—I was whisked away to exotic places I could only revisit in dreams.

The Revlon ads were especially wonderful. But there was only one problem—not one ad in those days featured a woman of color like me. Still, there was a "whisper of wisdom" inside me, telling me that someday my dream would come true and I would have a career in the cosmetics industry.

Very few companies bothered to market cosmetics to women of color in those days, but my inspiration came from C. J. Walker, the first African-American woman to become a millionaire. She started out with two dollars and a dream, right in my own hometown. She earned the fortune at the turn of the century,

---

① fascinate ['fæsə,net] v. 使着迷；使神魂颠倒

② incredible [ɪn'krɛdəbəl] a. 难以置信的；惊人的

美丽语录

Everything you want in life has a price connected to it. There's a price to pay if you want to make things better, a price to pay just for leaving things as they are, a price for everything.

—Harry Browne

生活里你想要的每样东西都有代价。如果你想让事情更好就要付出代价，仅让事情维持它们现况也要付出代价，每件事都有代价。

——哈利·布朗

从我记事时起，我就一直着迷于美丽的事物。作为一名被印第安纳波利斯千篇一律的玉米田包围的年轻女孩，充满时尚和化妆品的精彩世界与我毫不相干。每当我看到女性杂志上的广告——广告上那光彩夺目的模特拥有无瑕的肌肤、精湛的化妆技术，身着极度时髦的服装尽显线条优美的身姿——我都会被带到只有在梦里才能见到的外面的世界。

露华浓的广告尤其好。但是只存在一个问题：那时候的广告上没有像我这样有色人种的女性。但是，在我的内心有个声音，就是“智慧之音”，它告诉我说，总有一天我会梦想成真，我会在化妆品行业有所成就。

那时候，很少有公司卖化妆品给有色人种的女性，但是 C.J. 沃克激励着我，她是第一位成为百万富翁的非洲裔美国女性。她就在我的家乡，凭借着 2 美元和一个梦想发家致富。她通过向同她一样的女性销售护发产品，在本世纪初赚得了财富。

with her own line of hair-care products just for women like herself.

I graduated from college with a degree in public health education. Before long I got a job with a leader in the pharmaceuticals industry—and became the first African-American woman to sell pharmaceuticals in Indiana. People were shocked that I took the job because a woman of color selling encyclopedias in my territory had just been killed. In fact, when I started, the physicians I dealt with looked at me as if I had two heads.

But eventually my uniqueness worked to my advantage. The doctors and nurses remembered me. And I reversed the negative halo effect by doing the job better than other people. Along with pharmaceuticals, I sold them Girl Scout cookies and helped the nurses with their makeup. They began to look forward to my coming, not just for the novelty, but because we enjoyed such heartwarming visits.

Within two years, I'd broken **numerous**[①] sales records and was recognized as a Distinguished Sales Representative, formerly an all-white male club. I was looking forward to some hard-earned commission checks when suddenly, the company decided to subdivide the region and hired a handsome blond man to take my place. He would enjoy the fruits of my labor, while I was reassigned to another area that needed a lot of work. At this point, my dream of that cosmetics career with Revlon seemed a million miles away.

Discouraged and disenchanted, I picked up and moved to Los Angeles. Then one Sunday, as I searched longingly through the ads in the Los Angeles Times, there it was: a classified ad for a regional manager job with Revlon. I lit up completely and dove for the phone first thing Monday morning. The voice at the other end said that due to overwhelming response, Revlon was taking no

① numerous ['numərəs] a. 许多的，很多的

我以公共卫生教育学位从大学毕业。不久，我在一家医药行业的领头公司获得了一份工作，成为了在印第安纳州销售药物的第一位非洲裔美国女性。人们对于我得到这份工作表示很吃惊，因为在这一地区刚有一位有色人种女性因为卖百科全书而被杀。事实上，当我开始工作时，与我打交道的内科医生看我就仿佛我是个有两个头的怪物。

最终，我的独特性成为了我的优势。医生和护士都记得我。而且，通过这份工作，我比其他人更能消除别人对我们的成见。卖药的同时，我还向女童子军出售饼干，帮助护士化妆。她们开始盼望着我来，不是因为这些新奇廉价的小物品，而是因为我们很享受这样交心的相处。

两年间，我打破了许多次销售记录，在以前都是白种男人的团队里，我被认为是杰出的销售代表。正在我期望着辛苦所得的销售佣金时，公司突然决定划分销售区域，聘任了一名帅气的金发男人接替我的位置。他可以享受我的劳动成果，而我却要被分配到另一区域并要重新做很多工作。此时此刻，关于露华浓化妆品的梦想离我似乎十万八千里远。

万分沮丧和大失所望的我收拾行李去了洛杉矶。然而，在一个星期天，当我在《洛杉矶时报》的广告上渴望地搜寻信息时，我看到了一个分类广告刊登招聘露华浓地区经理的消息。一瞬间，我的整个人亮了，星期一早上的第一件事就是打电话。电话那头的人说，由于收到太多回复，现在他

more resumes.

I was devastated. But then a dear friend said to me, "Marilyn, I know you aren't going to let this job slip through your fingers. Go on down there anyway." Suddenly inspired and determined to turn the challenge into an adventure, I drove down to the Marriott where they were conducting interviews. When I arrived, a desk clerk curtly informed me that there was no way I could get an interview, nor would Mr. Rick English take my resume. I walked away, smiling. At least I now had the name of the man I needed to see.

I decide to have lunch to listen for the whisper of wisdom that would provide me with a new strategy. Sure enough, the idea came to me to explain my situation to the cashier as I was about to leave the restaurant. She immediately picked up the phone to find out what room Mr. English was in. "Room 515," she said turning to me. My heart began to pound.

I stood outside room 515, said a prayer, and knocked on the door. The minute he opened the door I said, "You haven't met the best person for the job because you haven't talked to me yet."

He looked stunned and said, "Wait a minute until I finish this interview and I'll speak to you." When I entered the room, I was clear and firm that this job was for me, and I got the job.

My first day at Revlon was like a dream come true. They hired me to market a new line of hair-care products designed especially for people of color. And by the time I'd worked there three years, the public was beginning to demand natural, cruelty-free products.

With public sentiment on my side, here was my chance! Once again listening to the whisper of wisdom inside me, I opened my own cosmetics company, which to this day continues to give me a sense of fulfillment impossible

们公司已经不再接收简历了。

我整个人立刻就蔫了。但是，我的一个好朋友对我说："玛里琳，我知道你不会就这样让这份工作从眼前溜走的。无论怎样，你要去他们公司看一下。"这句话瞬间激发了我，我决定冒险挑战一次，开车去他们的面试地点——万豪国际集团。当我到达那里时，接待员很无礼地告诉我，我不可能参加面试，瑞克·英格丽史先生也不会接收我的简历。我微笑着走开了，至少现在，我知道了我需要见的那个人的名字。

我决定去吃午饭，倾听我的智慧之音给我提供新战略。果真，在我将要离开餐厅时，我突然想到把我的情况告诉那个收银员。她马上拿起电话查看英格丽史先生的房间号。"515 房间。"她转身告诉我。我的心开始怦怦直跳。

我站在 515 房间的门外，祈祷了一下，然后敲门。在他开门的那一刻，我说道："你还没遇到最适合这份工作的人吧，那是因为你还没有和我交谈。"

他吃了一惊，说："你等一下，等我结束这个面试再和你谈。"在我进入房间时，我就清楚并坚信，这份工作就是我的了，确实，我也得到了。

我在露华浓公司工作的第一天，就仿佛我的梦成真了一样。他们任命我去销售新生产的特别为有色人种设计的护发产品。当我在露华浓工作三年后，公众开始追求自然、无刺激的产品。

当公众意见与我相同时，我知道我的机会来了！我再次听从了内心的智慧之音，开了自己的化妆品公司。直到今天，我的公司还一直给予我难

to describe.

I truly believe we should never give up on our hopes and dreams. The path may be rocky and twisted, but the world is waiting for that special contribution each of us was born to make. What it takes is the courage to follow those whispers of wisdom that guide us from inside. When I listen to that, I expect nothing less than a miracle.

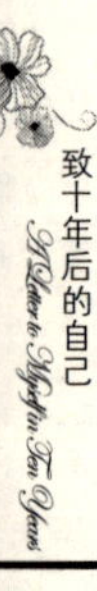

以形容的成就感。

我确实认为我们不应该放弃希望和梦想。成功之路也许崎岖，但是世界在期待我们每个人生而注定要为世界所做的贡献。你需要的就是有勇气跟随由内心发出的、指引我们的智慧之音。在你听从它后，你就只需要期待奇迹发生。

Chapter 4

写给未来的自己

Tomorrow is the most important thing in life. Comes in to us at midnight very clean. It's perfect when it arrives and it puts itself in our hands, and hopes we've learned something from yesterday.

——John Wayne

明天是生命里最重要的东西。午夜时它纯洁无暇地来临，然后完美地把自己交到我们手中，并希望我们已经从昨天学有所成。

——约翰·韦恩

Bend, but Don't Break

弯曲，但不折断

© Ralph Manuel

One of my fondest memories as a child is going by the river and sitting idly on the bank. There I would enjoy the peace and quiet, watch the water rush downstream, and listen to the chirps of birds and the rustling of leaves in the trees. I would also watch the bamboo trees bend under pressure from the wind and watch them return gracefully to their upright or original position after the wind had died down.

When I think about the bamboo tree's ability to bounce back or return to it's original position, the word **resilience**① comes to mind. When used in reference to a person this word means the ability to readily recover from shock, depression or any other situation that stretches the limits of a person's emotions.

Have you ever felt like you are about to snap? Have you ever felt like you are at your breaking point? Thankfully, you have survived the experience to live to talk about it.

During the experience you probably felt a mix of emotions that threatened your health. You felt emotionally drained, mentally exhausted and you most likely endured unpleasant physical symptoms.

① resilience [ri'ziliəns] n. 适应力；弹性

美丽语录

The two most powerful warriors are patience and time.

—Leo Tolstoy

时间与耐心是最强大的两个战士。

——列夫·托尔斯泰

孩提时代最美好的记忆，莫过于独自来到河边，悠闲地坐在河岸上。在那里，我可以深深陶醉在平静和安宁中，看河水奔涌着向下游流去，听小鸟唧唧喳喳地歌唱，听树叶随风摇曳的沙沙声。我也会看着那竹子在风力作用下变得弯曲，而当风力逐渐减小时，又看它们优雅地回到原来直立的位置上。

当想起竹子可以反弹回到原来的位置上时，“韧性”这个词出现在我的脑海里。引用这个词来形容某个人，它的意思就是指此人从震惊、沮丧或任何其他产生强烈情绪的情况中迅速复苏的能力。

你是否曾经觉得自己就要垮掉？你是否曾感觉自己已濒临崩溃的边缘？值得庆幸的是，你从这些经历中幸存下来，现在还活着并且还能谈论它们。

在这些经历中，你也许感觉到混杂的情感对你的健康产生了威胁。你感觉情绪低落，精神疲惫，而且你还很可能忍受着极不舒服的身体症状。

Life is a mixture of good times and bad times, happy moments and unhappy moments. The next time you are experiencing one of those bad times or unhappy moments that take you close to your breaking point, bend but don't break. Try your best not to let the situation get the best of you.

A measure of hope will take you through the unpleasant **ordeal**[①]. With hope for a better tomorrow or a better situation, things may not be as bad as they seem to be. The unpleasant ordeal may be easier to deal with if the end result is worth having.

If the going gets tough and you are at your breaking point, show resilience. Like the bamboo tree, bend, but don't break!

① ordeal [ɔ:'di:əl] n. 严酷的考验；痛苦的经验

生活中有顺境也有逆境，有快乐时光，也有悲伤时刻。下次，当你处于逆境或悲伤时刻并临近崩溃极限时，记得像竹子一样，弯下身去但不倒下。你要竭尽所能，不被困难打倒。

适当的希望将会让你经受住严酷的考验。希望明天会更好或希望状况会好转，可以使事情不像看起来那么糟糕。如果最终的结果是值得付出的，那么不愉快的苦难也许会更容易应付一些。

假如生活异常艰难，直把你逼向崩溃的边缘，请你展现出韧性，就像竹子一样，可以弯曲，但不会折断！

Stutter

口吃

© Madison G., Alhambra, CA

My name is M-m-m-adison. That has always been a particularly difficult word for my lips to form, especially on unexpected occasions. In my mind I know exactly what I want to say and when and how I want to say it, but every now and then my words **stumble**① out in repetitive prolonged syllables accompanied by grimacing and pursed lips in a futile attempt to "push" the words out.

I have coped with stuttering my entire life, a problem that often goes unnoticed by those around me since I possess this speech **impediment**② to a very limited degree and experience it only in certain situations. However, it has wielded the same impact on my life as if I had it to its full extent. There have been times when I have wanted to rip my vocal cords from my throat in frustration, not understanding why I cannot speak with ease like those around me.

For many years I have worn a mask, one giving the appearance of fluency and normalcy. I've made a relatively successful attempt to hide my stutter, assuming the world had no desire to hear flawed or imperfect speech. I've kept it hidden by avoiding situations where I run the risk of stuttering. I have

---

① stumble ['stʌmbəl] v. 踌躇，蹒跚；失足；犯错

② impediment [ɪm'pedɪmənt] n. 口吃；妨碍；阻止

美丽语录

The best day of your life is the one on which you decide your life is your own. No apologies or excuses. No one to lean on, rely on, or blame.

—Bob Moawad

人生最美好的事莫过于决定过自己的人生，没有歉疚或借口，也不倚靠、依赖或责怪他人。

——鲍勃·莫瓦德

我叫曼——曼——曼——迪逊。对我来说，这一直是很难发音的三个字，尤其是在突发情况下。我的大脑清楚地知道我想说什么、什么时候说以及怎么说这几个字，但是在发这些字的音时，我常常会反复地延长这个字，并且伴随着狰狞的表情和撅起的嘴唇，我努力地想“挤出”这几个字来，但却做不到。

我一生都在对付我的口吃问题，因为我的言语障碍问题程度很轻，而且只会在某些情景下才会出现，所以我的口吃问题经常被我身边的人忽略。然而，这对我生活造成的影响就如同我是个严重的言语障碍者一样大。在失望沮丧的时候，我有好几次都想撕裂喉咙里的声带，我不明白，为什么我不能像身边的人一样自然地说话。

多年来，我一直带着面具生活，给别人一种我说话很流利正常的表面感觉。我也相当成功地努力隐瞒了我的口吃问题，因为我觉得世人不愿意听到有缺陷或不完美的说话。我一直避免会让我陷入口吃问题的情况来隐瞒这个事实。而且我总是努力地让自己生活的其他方面都能尽其完美，以

always striven for perfection in all other areas of my life, futilely attempting to compensate for my problem.

I exhausted myself. The obsessive drive that fueled my determination to shut out and ignore a festering disability started to corrode me from the inside out. The lies and deception usually strangled and suffocated me more than my stuttering ever did during a block or period of disfluency. Denial was the crutch upon which I rested, an unstable one that finally gave way this past year. I reached a breaking point, unable to withstand the pressure of pretending to be somebody I was not. After years of refusing to seek help, I was forced to acknowledge that there was, in fact, a problem.

My speech therapist extended her hand to me, hoisting me up. She is a woman who stutters severely herself but is unashamed and unapologetic when speaking at her achingly slow pace. She stumbles over certain words and at times experiences difficulties, yet perseveres through each sentence.

Entering her office that first time, we watched a videotape of her giving a speech in a college class, neck craned and grimacing, stuttering uncontrollably for ten minutes straight. It reminded me of me. I had never identified with anyone like I did with her in that moment. I discovered that I really wasn't alone after all.

Her office is a sanctuary, a place where I will not be judged for my imperfect speech. It's a safe heaven where I won't receive curious or impolite stares from those who don't understand what it's like to struggle with the simplest daily task—a place where I can stutter to my heart's content.

I've finally found my way. I accept that I have this disability and consider myself blessed to be a stutterer. I feel privileged to be among those who are disabled because we are able to appreciate certain abilities normally taken for granted. We know what it's like at times to find ourselves without them.

此来试着弥补我的这个问题，但一切都是徒然。

我感到筋疲力尽。这强迫性的内驱力使我耗尽了决心，让我忽视了自己严重的缺陷，并开始由内而外地折磨我。比起不流利的口吃问题，谎言和欺骗更是经常让我痛苦地窒息。否认是我依靠的拐杖，但它却不稳固，最终在过去的一年里夭折了。我到达了一个转折点，我不再忍受着假装某个不是我自己的个人压力。在我多年拒绝寻求帮助之后，我不得不承认，我确实有个问题。

我的言语治疗师向我伸出了友善之手，她给了我很大的鼓舞。她是个本身口吃就很严重的女性，但对于自己那令人痛苦的缓慢的语速，她丝毫不感到羞愧和抱歉。她会在某些字词上结巴，有时也会很吃力，但是她始终坚持一句句地说完。

第一次到她的办公室时，我们观看了她在一个大学教室里演讲的录像带。她伸着脖子、露出狰狞的表情，无法控制地口吃，做了整整十分钟的演讲。这让我想起了我自己，我从没有像那一刻一样，与别人产生如此这般的共鸣。我发现，口吃确实不只是我一个人才有的问题。

她的办公室像是一块圣地，在那里，我不会因为我有瑕疵的言语而被别人品头论足。那是一个避风港，在那里，不会有人向我投来好奇或不礼貌的目光。这些人不懂得每天与最简单的日常口语挣扎是什么感觉。在那里，我可以尽情结结巴巴地说话。

我终于找到了自己。我接受了我的缺陷，并认为自己是因为受祝福而成为个结巴。我庆幸自己成为有缺陷的一员，因为这样，我们通常就会对拥有一些别人都想当然的能力而感激。因为我们知道，在寻找真实自己的路上，如果没有它们将会是什么模样。

Don't Let Anger Get the Best of You

管理你的愤怒情绪

◎ Winifred Yu Walking

You're late for a job interview when traffic slows to a crawl. At the supermarket, a customer wheeling a full cart cuts ahead of you in the express check-out line. You spend months on a make-it or break-it project, and your lazy colleague lands the promotion.

Feel that burn? Before you implode with rage or erupt into a **tantrum**①, take a deep breath and remember this: Anger hurts. Study after study has found that high levels of anger and hostility are associated with greater risk for heart disease, poor immune responses, and even a **propensity**② for obesity. Men with high anger scores were three times more likely to develop heart disease than their calmer cohorts, a Harvard School of Public Health study found. And in women, arguments with spouses raise hormone levels and lower immunity—a real problem, since lower immune response may boost women's risk of cancer.

Anger unleashes a torrent of hormones that wreak **havoc**③ on our circulatory and immune systems. When we are angry, our fight-or-flight response prompts

---

① tantrum ['tæntrəm] n. 发脾气，发怒
② propensity [prə'pensiti] n. 倾向；习性
③ havoc ['hævək] n. 大破坏；混乱

美丽语录

Character may be manifested in the great moments, but it is made in the small ones.

—Phillips Brooks

性格往往在重大时刻显现出来，但它却是平日点滴培养起来的。

——菲利普·布鲁克斯

交通通行速度缓慢，而你赶着去参加一个面试，你已经迟到了。超市里，一名顾客推着一整车东西，在快速结账通道插队到你前面。你在一个事关公司命运的项目上花了几个月时间辛勤工作，而懒惰的同事却升了职。

感觉怒火中烧吗？在你火冒三丈而大发雷霆之前，请做一次深呼吸并牢记：愤怒会带来伤害。多项研究发现，极度愤怒和敌意情绪可能会使患心脏病的几率更大，让免疫系统更脆弱，甚至导致肥胖的可能。哈佛大学公共卫生学院的研究发现，经常极度愤怒的男性患心脏病的几率比心绪平静的研究对象要高三倍。对女性而言，与配偶争吵会提高激素水平，降低免疫力——这是一个真正严重的问题，因为较低水平的免疫反应可能会增加女性患癌症的风险。

愤怒释放了大量荷尔蒙，这会严重影响我们的循环系统和免疫系统。当我们生气时，我们的“战斗或逃跑”反应提示肾上腺迅速分泌出额外的肾上腺素和皮质醇。这两种激素会导致心率加快、血压飙升，免疫系统工

our adrenal glands to send out an extra jolt of adrenaline and cortisol. The two hormones then cause the heart rate to speed up, blood pressure to soar, and the immune system to slow down—all helpful responses if you're going to fight or flee, but not if you're going to stand and seethe.

The extra hormones also cause blood platelets to clump and fat cells to empty into the bloodstream. Then, when the extra energy isn't used, the liver converts the fat into cholesterol. Extra cholesterol creates plaque in the arterial walls, which, over time, raises the risk for heart disease. To make matters worse, hostile people are more likely to overeat, smoke, and drink too much alcohol, studies have found.

It doesn't seem to matter whether you release the anger or hold it in, experts say. The effects on your health are the same. "Anger is anger," says Redford Williams, M.D., director of the Behavioral Medicine Research Center at Duke University Medical Center and co-author of the book Life Skills. "Both are harmful to health."

The good news is, it is possible to control your anger. "By evaluating it and using various techniques, you can talk yourself out of it," Williams says. "That's what's nice about us humans: We can always do something or not do something to change our behavior."

Take stock

Many people who are angry don't recognize themselves as angry, according to Knoxville psychologist Richard Driscoll. He suggests that you ask yourself these questions to measure your anger **quotient**[①]: Do you feel as if you are frequently mistreated by others? Do you often consider minor inconveniences

① quotient ['kwəuʃənt] n. 份额

作得更缓慢——如果你要去“战斗或逃跑”，所有这些反应都是有益的；但如果你要去与人对峙或变得十分激动，那这些反应却是有害的。

额外分泌的荷尔蒙也会引起血小板凝结，脂肪细胞会趁机流入血液中。进而，当额外的能量没有被消耗掉时，肝脏会将脂肪转化为胆固醇。额外的胆固醇会在血管壁上产生斑块。随着时间的推移，就会增加罹患心脏病的风险。更糟糕的是，研究发现，内心充满敌意的人有可能吃得过多，或更可能吸烟、酗酒。

专家认为，将愤怒释放出来或将其掩藏在心里似乎并没有太大区别，两者对健康的影响是相同的。“愤怒就是愤怒，”杜克大学医学中心行为医学研究中心主任、《生活技能》合著者雷德福·威廉姆斯博士说道，“两者都有害健康。”

好消息是，控制愤怒是可能的。“通过评估它，使用各种技术，你可以说服自己摆脱愤怒情绪，”威廉姆斯说。“这就是我们人类厉害的地方：我们总是可以做点什么或不做什么来改变我们的行为。”

作出评估

诺克斯维尔的心理学家理查德·德里斯科尔说，许多愤怒发火的人都没有意识到自己在生气。他建议问自己以下问题来判断是否发怒：你是否觉得经常被别人虐待呢？你经常把轻微不便视作对你的个人攻击吗？你经

to be personal attacks against you? Do you complain often? Do you exaggerate the actions of others or take their **affronts**[①] personally? On the road, do you frequently curse other drivers, to the point that driving has become unpleasant?

Keep a record

Many people are unaware of what ticks them off, says Jerry Deffenbacher, Ph.D., a professor of psychology at the University of Colorado in Fort Collins. "For lots of us, our anger sort of happens," he says. "We don't know what it comes from. We're just on automatic pilot."

To get a better sense of what makes you mad, keep a journal of situations that **rile**[②] you. Reflect on why they set you off and make you feel wronged. Ask yourself honestly whether your anger is justified. By writing down feelings and situations, you'll become more aware of the events that get your ire and maybe even avoid them.

Change or accept

When you feel anger welling up, take a change-it or accept-it approach. If, for example, your neighbor's garbage is fluttering into your yard yet again, it's time to put your problem-solving skills into motion. Calmly discuss the situation, and look for ways to change it.

If you can't do anything about the situation—the rude driver who just cut you off has left the scene—work to put your anger on hold right then and there. Accept that you can't do anything about it, take some deep breaths, and move on to something else.

---

① affronts [ə'frʌnt] n. 侮辱

② rile [rail] v. 激怒

常抱怨吗？你会夸大他人的行为或把他人的侮辱视为故意针对你的攻击吗？在路上时你经常诅咒其他司机，而使开车变得很不愉快吗？

做好记录

科罗拉多大学柯林斯堡分校的心理学教授杰里·德芬巴赫博士说，很多人都不知道是什么东西惹他们发怒。“对于我们很多人，愤怒似乎是自然而然发生的，”他说，“我们不知道愤怒的来源，它总是自动发挥作用。”

为了更好地了解是什么惹你生气，把激怒你的场景记录在日记里。反思为什么这些场景会激怒你，让你觉得委屈。诚实地问问自己，你的愤怒是否有道理。通过写下自己的感情和经历情况，你更容易意识到让你愤怒的事件，甚至可以更有效地避免它们。

改变或者接受

当你感到越来越愤怒时，采取一种“改变或接受”的态度。比如，假设你邻居的垃圾又飞进你家院子，这时你应该采取解决问题的态度，平静地与对方讨论问题，寻找方法来改变它。

有些情况下，你无计可施——比如，粗鲁无礼的司机插队到你前面，如果他已经离开——那你应该试图把愤怒控制在当时的现场。学会接受你什么也做不了这个事实，做几次深呼吸，把注意力转移到别的东西上面。

Don't take it personally

How many times have you said to yourself, "That shouldn't have happened to me" or "I don't deserve that"? Such thinking can easily set off angry feelings. But smart people realize that, sometimes, the water-on-the-back-of-a-duck approach is the best way to deal with many of life's unfairnesses.

"Many of us have a God-like or little-kid-like mentality that we shouldn't be imposed upon, frustrated, or have things happen to us," Deffenbacher says. "That's a demanding kind of thinking. Fact is, you're going to have your base rate of crummy things happen to you." The better able you are to accept that, the less angry you'll be.

Stop dwelling on the past

If you still remember a minor infraction long after it happened, it's time to let go. Life has moved on, and so should you. Practice understanding people who have dealt you minor wrongs. Think of the problem as having been caused by the situation, not the person. If it's a more serious matter, such as childhood abuse or an unfaithful spouse, consider seeing a therapist to help you work through and release the pain, says Susan Heitler, Ph.D., a psychologist in Denver.

Adjust your routine

If you've been keeping track of your anger, you know what sets you off. Use that information to avoid upsetting situations. For instance, if you know that the grocery store is crowded on weekends, shop after work. By avoiding frustrating situations, you dodge anger.

Ultimately, the ways you react to upsetting situations and express your

不要对号入座

你会经常对自己说“这不应该发生在我身上”或“我不应该有这样的境遇”吗？这种想法很容易引发愤怒情绪。但是，聪明的人会认识到，有时候“常在河边走，哪有不湿鞋”的自我解释，是处理众多人生不公最好的态度和方法。

“许多人都有一种神般或孩子般的心态，觉得我们不应该被强迫，不应该遭受挫折或沮丧情绪，或不应该有不好的事情发生到我们头上，”德芬巴赫博士说。“这是一个要求极高的想法。事实是，对坏事情发生在你身上的基本概率，你心里必须要有相应的预期。”你越能接受这一事实，就会越少生气。

不要总是沉湎于过去

如果你还记得已经过去很久的一次小挫折，那么是时候释怀了。生活在继续，你应该继续前行。试着理解那些待你不公的人。把问题看成是当时的情况造成的，而不是某个人造成的。丹佛的心理学家苏珊·海特勒博士说，如果那是一个比较严重的问题，比如虐待儿童或伴侣不忠，可以考虑让心理治疗师帮你度过难关、释放痛苦。

调整你的生活习惯

如果你一直在追踪你的愤怒来源，你就知道什么会让你发怒。使用这些信息来避免容易让你发怒的情况。例如，假如你知道通常杂货店在周末会非常拥挤，那么你可以在下班后去购物。通过避免令人沮丧的情境，你

anger come from a combination of several factors, including **genetics**[1], upbringing, and culture. Your response also varies by day, depending on your mood and even how tired you are.

Fortunately, angry people can learn to become happy people. "We just have this personality type that sometimes gets us into trouble," Williams says. "You'll always have that tendency to get angry. But you can probably control it enough to keep it from damaging your health."

① genetics [dʒi'netiks] n. 遗传学

可以避开愤怒情绪。

总之，你对让人不快的情境的反应方式，以及你表达不满的方式，都来自于以下几个因素的组合，包括遗传学、养育过程和文化因素。你每一天的反应可能也不尽相同，这取决于你的情绪，甚至是当天你的疲惫程度。

幸运的是，愤怒的人们可以学会成为快乐的人。“这种易怒的人格类型有时会给我们带来麻烦，”威廉姆斯说，“你总是会有生气的倾向。但是你可以控制它，让它不至于伤害你的健康。”

Standing Tall on a Surfboard in Midlife

中年冲浪第一课

© Mike Gordon

A wave rose behind me, but it was barely a swell. If I had been standing instead of lying on a surfboard, it might have been tall enough to **splash**① my calves.

Still, I stroked the water like a man about to be swallowed by a shark. If the board was moving, I couldn't tell. I started to think this was an awful idea, that maybe this was not meant to be.

Maybe I had waited too long to learn how to surf.

Middle-aged egos can be painful to watch. A man can turn forty, spot a few gray hairs and do all kinds of things to prove he's still younger. Some men have affairs with leggy redheads, others start jogging. I decided to make good on a promise I made to myself when I was twelve.

I was going to learn to surf.

I often told myself it wasn't right to have grown up in Hawaii and not have learned how to surf. All my life, this concept got steady reinforcement. Everywhere, I saw people with surfboards—young people, old people, men, women. Once, I saw a five-year-old "carving wave". Another time, I saw a dog

---

① splash [splæʃ] v. 溅（湿）；报道

美丽语录

You may avoid suffering and sorrow if you don't risk, but you simply cannot learn, feel, change, grow, love, live.

—Bob Proctor

若不冒险，或许你能避开苦难或哀伤，但你会因此而无法学习、感受、改变、成长、爱别人，以及生活。

——鲍勃·普罗克特

我身后涌起一阵波浪，但却远不是什么巨浪。如果我站在冲浪板上而不是躺在那里，它可能刚刚能溅到我小腿肚的高度。

然而，我战战兢兢地划过水面，仿佛马上就要被鲨鱼吞噬似的。我甚至无法分辨冲浪板是否在滑动。我开始觉得来学冲浪简直是个糟糕透顶的主意，或许，我根本就不应该来学。

也许，在学习冲浪之前，我等待了太长时间。

审视中年人的自我是非常痛苦的。一个人刚满 40 岁时，虽然头上冒出了几根白发，但他可以做各种各样的事情来证明自己依然年轻。一些男人与红头发的长腿姑娘们调调情，另外一些人则开始慢跑。而我则决定兑现自己在 12 岁时许下的诺言。

我要去学冲浪。

我经常告诉自己，在夏威夷长大而没有学会冲浪是一件极其丢人的事情。在我的一生中，这一观念不断得到稳步强化。到处都可以看到人们扛着冲浪板——年轻人、老年人、男人、女人。有一次，我看见一个 5 岁的孩子在玩“雕刻波浪”。还有一次，我甚至看见一只狗在“作十趾驾驭”。

"hang ten". How hard could it be to learn this?

And yet, I didn't do anything about it. Instead, I made excuses about not having enough time and not knowing anyone who would teach me.

Then I saw a yellow flyer for a surf school in Waikiki, and the child in me spoke up, telling me it was time.

That was how I found myself floating off Diamond Head at a surf break called Tonggs. My arms were stroking the water as if my life had no other purpose. The wave scooped me up as my instructor grabbed the back of my surfboard and gave me a quick **shove**① forward.

I was moving, but I wasn't surfing. Before I could persuade myself to react, the ride was over. I'd blown it on my first attempt.

My instructor didn't know what to make of this. Then he shoved my board toward shore so quickly, I thought he was angry. "Paddle, now!" he shouted.

What happened next didn't take long: I stood up. I fell down. The wave passed me by.

Each new wave generated the same result: a wipeout with all the grace of a drunken belly flop.

Another wave rose like a dare. And then it happened. It was over in twenty seconds, but I'll remember it forever. Even if it never happens again.

I'll remember the sky was slightly overcast, and the ocean was an **undulating**② slab of gray-blue, streaked with white breakers. I'll remember the taste of salt water on my lips and the ache between my shoulder blades.

But most of all, I'll remember that I stood up. I surfed.

---

① shove [ʃʌv] n. 推；挤

② undulating ['ʌndjə.letiŋ] a. 波状的

我不禁反问自己，学这个能有多难?

然而，我并没有马上采取行动。相反，我编造了很多借口，比如没有足够的时间、不知道谁可以教我等等。

后来我在怀基基海滩看到了一个冲浪学校的黄色传单。我心底那个孩子开始跟我开口说话，告诉我是时候去学冲浪了。

再然后，我便漂浮在钻石头山附近一个叫做唐格斯的冲浪圣地。我的双臂使劲地划着水，好像我的人生除此以外没有其他任何的目的。海浪袭来，把我高高地涌起。我的教练从背面一把抓住我的冲浪板，把我快速往前推。

我感觉自己在移动，但没在冲浪。我还没来得及说服自己做出反应，一切就结束了。我的第一次尝试失败了。

教练很难理解我的表现。然后，他把我的冲浪板快速推向岸边，我以为他生气了。“现在划啊！”他喊道。

接下来发生的事情倒很迅速：我站了起来，然后摔倒了。浪头越过我向前奔涌而去。

每个新的浪潮都产生了相同的结果：我一次又一次被浪打翻，优雅地露出圆鼓鼓的啤酒肚。

另一波浪头汹涌而来，仿佛要向我发起挑战。然后，难忘的事情发生了，尽管只有短短 20 秒就结束了，但我会永远记住这件事，即使它永远不会再发生。

我记得天空有些阴沉，海平面仿佛一块上下起伏的灰蓝色石板，夹杂着白色的碎浪。我记得嘴唇上盐水的味道，还有肩胛骨之间的阵阵疼痛。

但最重要的是，我会记住，那一刻我站起来了，我冲浪了。

The Greatest Gift We Can Give to Our Children

给孩子最珍贵的礼物

© Leslie Karen Lobell

This past year—and the soon to end Year of The Golden Dragon on the Chinese calendar (considered a very lucky year for bearing children)—seemed to bring a baby boom to many places, including my island home of Providenciales. On days when I am able to enjoy the luxury of morning coffee at a favorite outdoor café, I often see mothers carrying infants as young children run around the plaza, full of energy and excitement. Though not a mother myself, (I am a proud aunt of two bright and beautiful nieces), I cannot help but smile back at the beaming faces and feel the tug these young girls and boys have on my heartstrings. I always pray that these young ones will hold onto their exuberance: the passion and curiosity with which they approach life.

Children are so full of joy, hopes, and dreams. They are spontaneous and creative. Sometimes they say or do things that make adults burst into laughter (or occasionally lead a parent to feel embarrassed), because we recognize that the child has not yet learned a particular rule of social etiquette. There is something so wonderful about how young children are directly connected to their essence, before the lessons and the inevitable pain of life experience lead them to hide that essence under layers of protection.

美丽语录

Most people are other people. Their thoughts are someone else's opinions, their lives a mimicry, their passions a quotation.

—Oscar Wilde

大部分人过着他人的生活，他们的想法是别人的看法，他们的人生是个仿制品，他们的热忱出自一句名言。

——奥斯卡·王尔德

过去这一年——即将结束的这一年，中国农历金龙年（被认为是生育孩子的幸运年份）——似乎给许多地方带来一个婴儿潮，包括我家所在的普罗维登西亚莱斯岛。当我在最喜爱的户外咖啡馆享受奢侈的早间咖啡时，我经常看到妈妈们抱着婴儿，身边年幼的孩子在广场上兴奋欢快地奔跑。虽然我自己不是一个母亲（我有两个聪明又漂亮的侄女，并为她们感到骄傲），我也忍不住朝着孩子们喜气洋洋的面孔微笑，并总能感觉到这些年幼的男孩女孩们在拨动着我的心弦。我一直祈祷，这些孩子们能一直保留他们的活力：对生活总是充满激情和好奇。

孩子们身上总是充满欢乐、希望和梦想，而且他们天性自然，并极具创造力。有时他们说或做的一些事情，往往引来大人的哄堂大笑（或偶尔让家长感到尴尬），因为我们意识到，这个孩子还没有学会社交礼仪中的特定规则。年幼孩子的美妙之处就在于本质的自然流露。这种本质，在他们遭受了屡次教训和不可避免的痛苦经历后，便会被他们隐藏保护起来。

As a therapist, often my job is to get people back in touch with that essence. They have buried it so well, so carefully, that they cannot even find it themselves. Getting in touch with that essence, and allowing it to show again, is inextricably linked to self-love. When we love ourselves, we love our core, our essence, and we bring forth more of that vital part of ourselves into our daily lives. It probably would not be an exaggeration to say that over 95% of the problems that clients bring to therapy—be it relationship problems, depression and anxiety, substance abuse, career indecision, or general dissatisfaction with one's personal or professional life—have some link (often a primary one) to a lack of self-love. This lack of self-love generally begins in childhood. When teenagers or adults walk into my office for counseling, I often think, "If only we could catch them sooner…"

To develop self-love, children need to know that they are loved, unconditionally. Many children fear they will be "kicked out" or abandoned if they do not behave in ways that please their parents. Children need to know that their parents love them, even when the parents do not approve of the child's behavior. Children need **consistency**① from their parents: They need to feel that they are on a solid foundation, and that their place in the family is secure. Children need both to see the actions and hear the words to reassure them of their parents' love. A big birthday gift from a parent who never says, "I love you" can feel like a bribe to a child. Similarly, when a parent forgets to pick up the child from school or doesn't plan anything special for the child's birthday, the child may hear an "I love you" from that parent as empty words. Many parents assume that their children "just know" that they love them, when this is not always the case.

---

① consistency [kən'sistənsi] n. 连贯，一致性，强度，硬度，浓稠度

作为一个临床医学家，通常我的工作是使人们恢复与这一本质的连结。他们小心翼翼地把它埋藏得那么深，甚至自己也没法找到它。恢复与本质的接触，并允许它再次显现，与自爱有着千丝万缕的联系。当我们爱自己的时候，我们爱自己的核心，即我们的本质，我们会将更多的本质融入日常生活。可以毫不夸张地说，前来接受治疗的客户身上超过 95% 的问题——可能是关系问题、抑郁和焦虑、毒品滥用、职业决策困难，或一般的对个人或职业生活的不满——与缺乏自爱（通常是首要关联）都有一定的联系。这种缺乏自爱通常始于儿童。当青少年和成年人走进我的办公室咨询时，我常常想，“如果我们能早点发现他们的话……”

要让孩子们自爱，必须先让孩子们知道他们是无条件被爱的。许多孩子都害怕，如果他们的行为举止让父母感觉不悦，他们会被“赶出去”或被遗弃。不论父母是否赞成他们的行为，孩子们都需要知道他们的父母爱他们。孩子需要从父母身上感受到一种连续性：他们需要感觉到自己有一个坚实的基础，他们在家里的位置是安全的。孩子们需要看到行动、听到话语来不断确认父母的爱。父母送给孩子一份丰厚的生日礼物，但从未向孩子说过“我爱你”，这感觉就像是贿赂孩子。同样，当父母忘记去学校接孩子或没有计划庆祝孩子生日，却对他们说“我爱你”时，他们就会觉得很空洞。许多父母想当然地认为孩子“知道”他们爱他，但事实并不总是如此。

一些人认为，最重要的是给予孩子“用钱买到最好的教育”。我不同意这种观点（虽然优秀的教育在我的列表上位置非常靠前）。我相信我们应该“教育好他们，让他们独立地走自己的路”。我们应该给我们的孩子尽可能

Some people believe that the most important thing to give a child is the "best education money can buy". I disagree (although an excellent education is very high on my list). I do believe we should "teach them well and let them lead the way". We should give our children the best education possible (both in and out of the classroom). We must share with them our sense of values and ethics, and encourage their curiosity to learn and explore on their own. Once we have given our children a solid foundation and the basic knowledge and tools they need, we need to let go and trust them to create their own lives, make their own mistakes, have their own successes, and follow their own **destiny**①. We need to let them blossom on their own. I think for many parents the greatest challenge is to learn how to give guidance and at the same time allow their children to be themselves, to have their own lives and follow their own dreams.

More important than giving a child a proper formal education is to foster the child's self-esteem. A child with a great education who lacks a sense of self-confidence and self-trust will rarely become a happy adult, whether or not he or she is "successful" in the material sense. However, a child who has grown to love himself or herself, will be motivated to learn or do whatever it takes to be successful and happy in life. As we must learn to love ourselves, so, too, must we encourage our children to love themselves, to trust their instincts and intuition, to know and express "the beauty they possess inside". If we give our children love that is unconditional, then they feel worthy of love; this is a key **ingredient**② for them to develop a sense of self-love. Therefore, I believe that unconditional love is the greatest gift we can give to our children.

---

① destiny['destini] n. 命运

② ingredient[in'gri:diənt] n. 成分，原料，配料，因素

好的教育（无论课内还是课外）。我们必须与他们分享我们的价值观和道德规范，并鼓励他们的好奇心去独立学习和探索。一旦我们给了孩子坚实的基础以及他们需要的基本知识和工具，我们要做的就是放手，并相信他们，让他们去创造自己的生活，让他们去犯错、去成功，经受他们自己的命运。我们需要让他们自己去开花结果。我觉得对许多父母来说，最大的挑战是学会如何给予指导，同时允许孩子做真正的自己，有自己的生活，并追求自己的梦想。

比起给孩子提供适当的正规教育，更重要的是培养孩子的自尊。一个接受了优良教育却缺乏自信心的孩子，成年后很难成为一个快乐的人，无论他或她在物质上是否“成功”。然而，一个已经学会爱自己的孩子，会主动地学习或行动以获得成功与幸福。我们必须学会爱自己，同样，我们必须鼓励我们的孩子爱自己，要让他们相信自己的本能和直觉，也要让他们知道和表达“自己拥有的内在美”。如果我们给孩子的爱是无条件的，他们就会觉得自己值得被爱；这是自爱养成的关键成分。因此，我相信，无条件的爱是我们可以给孩子的最伟大的礼物。

A Letter to Myself 10 Years Down the Road

致十年后的自己的一封信（一）

◎ Red

Dear Red,

You've been with hubby for 19 years now…are we happily celebrating our 15th anniversary? Do you still snuggle in the mornings before work or give each other head massages when you're stressed? Do you still make each other laugh? Does he still refuse to let you cook the main meals because he "fears death", oh, and does he still over-compliment your sandwiches in an attempt to get you to make them instead? Most importantly, are you two still in love?

If you answered no to any of these, you should work on that. Laugh more. Loosen up. Unless of course he did something supremely **crappy**[①]. Then you should…never mind…leave no proof.

So, did we change our minds on the kid front? If we didn't, do we have more dogs? If we did, I hope he or she is healthy and not a pain-in-the-butt like you were. I would hate for Mom to have been right. You know any kid you have is going to be a smart-ass, right? I wouldn't have it any other way. Is hubby a great dad? I bet he surprised himself.

How is our money looking? Did BFS take off? Is the house paid off as planned? Did hubby talk you into trading up yet? I hope not. Stick to your

① crappy ['kræpi] a. <俚>蹩脚的；没价值的；讨厌的

美丽语录

The purpose of our lives is to give birth to the best which is within us.

—Marianne Williamson

我们生活的目的是发现自己身上最好的内在品质。

——玛丽安娜·威廉森

亲爱的红：

你现在与老公在一起已经 19 年了……你们是否正在甜蜜地庆祝结婚 15 周年纪念日呢？早上上班之前你们还会偎依在一起吗？压力很大时，你们还会给对方做头部按摩吗？你们还能让对方欢笑吗？他是否仍然不让你做正餐，因为他担心你做的难吃得“要死”？哦，还有，他是否仍然喜欢大肆赞美你做的三明治，以此引诱你来做呢？最重要的是，你们两个还相爱吗？

如果你对以上任何一个问题的回答是“不”，那么在那个问题上，你要努力了。多笑笑，放松自己。当然，除非他做了一些非常糟糕的事情。那么你应该……没关系……注意不要留下任何证据。

我们有没有改变关于孩子的想法呢？如果没有，我们养了更多的狗吗？如果我们有孩子了，我希望他或她是健康的，而不是像你一样令人头疼。我讨厌妈妈也许是正确的。你知道你的孩子一定会是一个聪明的讨厌鬼，对吗？对此我深信不疑。老公会是一个伟大的父亲吗？我相信他会是一个好爸爸，甚至好得让他自己都吃惊。

我们的财务状况如何呢？股票有没有飞涨？这所房子是否按计划付清按揭了？老公说服你购买大房子了吗？我希望没有。坚持你的立场，让他

guns and keep his mind off it. You know how…buy him some board games or something. (Haha, you didn't think that was what I was going to say.)

Anyway, are we still on track to retire in 15 more years? If not, why? I don't want to work into our 60's, do you?

Are you still a nice person? Have you made someone **random**[①] smile today? I hope we still have a good sense of humor. I also hope we still help others. If you haven't volunteered for a while, schedule that for this weekend. You know you want to and there are a ton of places that appreciate our time.

Okay, please make sure that you make the rest of our life fun. Love hubby some more, you know he's crazy about you. Make a silly joke or use that kid voice we always fall into. If you haven't been silly lately, man up and try it out. You know we love to laugh.

Sincerely,

Red at 27…the one who hopes we had a great 10 years…

That was fun. Do any of you have any comments or questions for your future selves?

① random ['rændəm] a. 任意的；随机的；随意的

把注意力转移开来。你知道该怎么做……给他买一些桌游什么的。(哈哈，你觉得我不会这么说吧。)

还有，我们有望在 15 年后退休吗？如果不能，为什么？我不想 60 多岁了还在工作，你呢？

你还是一个好人吗？你今天让别人微笑了吗？我希望我们仍然富有幽默感，也希望我们还会帮助别人。如果你有一段时间没去做志愿者了，这个周末安排一下吧。你知道你想去，有很多地方需要我们的服务呢。

好了，请你保证我们以后的生活总是充满乐趣。多爱老公一些，你知道他疯狂地爱着你。时不时说一个笨拙的笑话，或模仿一下孩子的声音，这种时候我们总是哈哈大笑。如果你最近没有犯蠢，勇敢尝试一下。你知道我们爱笑。

真诚的，

27 岁的红……希望我们有美好的 10 年……

这很有趣。你们对将来的自己做过任何评价或问过任何问题吗？

Where Do You See Yourself in 10 Years

致十年后的自己的一封信（二）

© Ninja

Dear Ninja,

Holy Crap. It's 2020! Are there flying cars? Do you have a robot maid? Has the world come to an end? I guess if it had, you wouldn't be able to tell me anyways.

Seriously though, you are pushing 35 right now which means A) you have gray hair on your head, or B) you are balding. Depressing stuff huh? I have a few matters of business that I need to discuss with you.

1) Girl Ninja:

Dude you have been married for 10 years now! Have you been honoring your wife? Loving her for her benefit and not yours? Have you told her you think she is beautiful today? If not, you have some serious business that needs to get taken care of, mister. In fact, why don't you stop reading this letter right now and call her to tell her how much you appreciate her. I assume you two have gone through some pretty major fights over the years, but I have faith that you both remain committed to love. Remember love is not a fight, but it's something worth fighting for.

亲爱的忍者：

见鬼，已经 2020 年了！有会飞的汽车吗？你有机器人女仆吗？世界末日已经来临了吗？我想，如果世界末日真的降临了，你大概也没办法来告诉我。

说正经的，你马上满 35 岁了，这意味着：你头上有灰白头发了，或者你开始秃顶了。很令人沮丧吧？我有一些重要的事情需要和你商量。

1. 女孩忍者

伙计，你已经结婚 10 年了！你尊重你的妻子吗？你重视她的利益而不是自己的吗？你今天跟她说过她很美吗？如果没有，那么，先生，你有一项很重要的事情需要处理。事实上，你为什么不停止阅读这封信而马上打电话给她，告诉她你是多么欣赏她？多年来你们两个经历了一些非常重大的斗争，但是我相信你俩始终忠贞于对彼此的爱情。要记住爱情不是一场斗争，但是值得通过斗争去争取。

2) Kids:

Barring no major medical complications, it's safe to assume you probably have at least 2 kids, hopefully all boys (only kidding…sort of). Are you sticking to your commitment to be a good dad? Does your job allow you to cut out early to catch your kids youth soccer game? If not, it's time for you to start looking for a new job. I, meaning you, refuse to work in an industry that overtakes my family life. Do not **compromise**① this. Ever.

3) Finances:

Do you remember that silly blog you started after you graduated college? No? You don't? It was Punch Debt In The Face. Remember how clever you thought you were when you came up with that name? While you are most likely no longer blogging, I do hope that you have been continually growing in your knowledge of personal finance. You are debt free right? I swear if you still have that stupid Sallie Mae loan there is going to be hell to pay. More important than your individual journey through personal finance, how has the walk with Girl Ninja been? Do you sit down and talk money at least once a month? Does she know how much money you all have in savings? I hope that you have tamed your intense passion for PF and found a way to communicate finances with Girl Ninja in a way that benefits the both of you.

4) Fun:

Seriously man, you better still have a sense of humor and an excitement about life. I know as you grow older your responsibilities increase, but that doesn't mean you can't have a good time. What have you done lately that has

① compromise ['kɔmprəmaiz] v. 妥协处理，危害，妥协，让步

2. 孩子们

如果没有严重的并发症，也许可以假设你可能至少有两个孩子，希望都是男孩（只是开玩笑……）。你是否坚持履行承诺，做了一个好父亲？你的工作允许你提前下班赶着去看孩子们的青年足球比赛吗？如果不是，你应该重新找一份工作了。我，也就是你，不允许工作过多地挤占家庭生活的时间。在这一点上不要妥协，永远不要妥协。

3. 财务方面

你还记得那个从学校毕业就开始写的愚蠢的博客吗？忘了吗？你真的忘了吗？就是那个叫“迎头痛击债务”的博客。还记得当初你想出这个名字时觉得自己很聪明吗？虽然你很可能不再写博客，但我希望你在个人理财方面不断有所长进。你没有债务，对吗？我发誓，如果你还有那愚蠢的学生贷款，那你将面临严重的后果。比你的个人财务状况更重要的是，你和女孩忍者的进展如何了？你们会每月至少有一次坐下来谈谈钱吗？她是否知道你们一共存了多少钱？我希望你已经驯服了自己对证券投资的激情，并找到了与女孩忍者就财务方面进行沟通的有益方式。

4. 生活乐趣

说正经的，伙计，你最好还是有幽默感，有对生活的激情。我知道，随着年龄的增长，你的责任也在不断增加。但这并不意味着你不能过得幸福开心。你最近做了什么让人兴奋的事情吗？以至于肾上腺激素加速分泌？你正在参与一些能让你微笑的事情吗？记得提醒自己在高中时曾被大家投票推举为最具幽默感的学生，我希望这个愚蠢的奖项仍然能每一天都

given you an **adrenaline**[1] rush? Are you involved in things that make you smile? Remember you were voted your high school's best sense of humor, I hope you still live up to that silly award every single day.

If you haven't succeeded in these four areas, you have fallen short of your life goals. This letter is a reminder, that the 24 year old you, had an expectation to live a fulfilling and rewarding life. If that is not the case at the time you are reading this, you only have yourself to blame.

Sincerely,

Your much younger and better looking self

P.S. You currently weigh 180lbs, if you are tipping the 200 mark I'm gonna come cut the excess baggage off of you.

① adrenaline [ə'drenəlin] n. 肾上腺素（使激动兴奋等）

名副其实。

如果你在这四方面没有取得成功，那你就没有实现自己的生活目标。这封信是一个提醒，24 岁的你，渴望过上充实、有意义的生活。如果读这篇文章时你尚未过上这样的生活，你只能怪自己了。

真诚的，

更年轻、更帅气的我

附言：现在的我重 180 磅，如果你即将突破 200 磅大关，我要来帮你瘦身，减掉超重的部分。

A Letter to Myself in 10 Years

致十年后的自己的一封信（三）

© Trent

Many, many people write letters to their past selves, advising their earlier selves to avoid mistakes that they've made. I thought it might be interesting to take the opposite approach and write myself a letter today to read on my fortieth birthday.

Dear Trent,

Today is your fortieth birthday. Your son is twelve years old, your daughter is ten years old, and you've been married for fifteen years. Right now, I can **scarcely**[①] believe that's possible. I don't know what frustrations and joys you will have experienced between now and then, but I just wanted to pop in with a little reminder of the things you value now, so that maybe you'll sit down and use your fortieth birthday as an opportunity to really look at your life and make sure that it's still centered around the things that you value.

I guess that's the first thing I want to say. Right now, take a few hours and set it aside to really reflect on your life. You probably don't remember the day to day realities of your life when your daughter was a newborn and your son was two, but you spent it working full time at a job and at two side businesses, plus you devoted time to your children and your wife, spent time on your hobbies, and still squeezed in a bit of time for reflection, too. The times in your life that

① scarcely ['skɛəsli] adv. 几乎不，简直不，刚刚，决不

很多很多人写信给过去的自我，给过去的自我提供建议以避免他们已经犯下的错误。但我觉得，采取相反的方法，在今天写下一封信，在 40 岁生日时再来读，这可能会很有趣。

亲爱的特伦特，

今天是你 40 岁的生日。你的儿子 12 岁，你的女儿 10 岁，你已经结婚 15 年了。现在的我几乎难以相信这一切。我不知道从现在起你会经历哪些挫折，拥有哪些欢乐，但我只是想出来提醒你，哪些是你现在珍视的东西。也许你会坐下来，利用你 40 岁生日这个机会来真正审视一遍自己的生活，并确保生活的核心仍然是那些你认为重要的东西。

我想这是我首先想说的。现在，拿出几个小时的时间来真正反思一下你的生活。你可能已经不记得女儿刚生下来、儿子才 2 岁时日复一日的生活细节了，但是你在工作中全力以赴，在双方企业里来回奔波，你投入大量时间去照顾和陪伴妻子孩子，你会花些时间在兴趣爱好上，然后仍要挤出一些时间来思考。生活中郁郁寡欢的时节，与没有花时间反思的时节一样，都是莫大的浪费。所以，现在拿出时间，去林子里走一走，想想你现

you've been **melancholic**[①] have been the same ones where you failed to take time to reflect on things. So, take that time right now. Go for a walk in the woods and think about where you're at right now.

When you get back, do these things.

Take that wonderful wife of yours, the mother of your children, into your arms, give her a kiss, look her straight in the eyes, and tell her that you love her. Right now, she is the emotional center of your life, and even if that has changed somewhat in the intervening ten years, let me assure you that right now, as I write this, she is the reason to get up in the morning. Don't let little **aggravations**[②] get in the way of things.

Give each of your children a hug, too. You and your wife used to spend every evening completely devoted to them, and they've likely grown into interesting people as well. You're probably wondering where the time went, and asking yourself when your son turned into a budding young man and your daughter transformed from a soft, snuggly little baby into a nuanced and thriving child. Hug them both, and don't let these last few years of their childhood slip past. Take some extra time to spend with them, and never hesitate to let them know that you love them.

Think about what you really want to do. Right now, I'm planning on spending much of my thirties making the strongest possible foundation I can for you, one of financial security for you and your wife and those kids. Why? So you can do some amazing things now. Go on a few deeply memorable vacations in the next few years. Take your family and visit every continent in the world. Do some things that will build your family's connections, but also enable your

---

① melancholic [ˌmelən'kɔlik] a. 忧郁的，忧郁症的

② aggravation [ˌægrəv'eiʃən] n. 更恶化，加厉，恼怒，恼人的事

在的境况。

当你回到家时，记得做以下几件事。

把你的好妻子，你孩子的母亲拥入怀中，给她一个吻，直接看着她的眼睛，告诉她你爱她。现在，她是你生命的情感中心。即使过去的 10 年里有些变化，那么让我向你保证，现在，当我写这篇文章的时候，她是我每天早起的理由。不要让小小的愤怒伤害了你们的感情。

也给每个孩子一个拥抱。你和你的妻子过去常常整夜整夜地照顾他们，而他们现在很可能已经长成有趣的小大人了。你可能很想知道，也常常会问自己时间都到哪里去了。你儿子长成了一个崭露头角的年轻男子，你女儿不再是从前那个细声细气、小鸟依人的小宝贝，她成了一个心思细腻、茁壮成长的孩子。拥抱他们，不要让他们童年的尾巴轻易溜走。拿出一些额外的时间来陪伴他们，毫不犹豫地让他们知道你爱他们。

认真思考什么是你真正想做的事情。现在，我正在计划在 30 多岁这些年里给你打下尽可能牢固的基础，一个为你、妻子、孩子提供财务安全的基础。为什么? 因为这样的话，你现在就可以去做一些美好的事情。在接下去的几年里，你可以去度假，为自己留下很多深刻难忘的美好回忆；带上家人去拜访世界上的每一个大陆；做一些事来加强家人之间的联系，帮助孩子们成长，体会新事物。在过去的几年里我一直很忧心，我怎样才能照顾好这些孩子。现在他们长大了，我的烦恼应该有所减轻，你可以腾出

children to grow and see new things. I've spent much of my time over the last few years worrying about how I will be able to take care of those children, but they're growing up now and the worry should be less, so use those resources you've got to experience some new things.

Right now, our family's plan is to build a new house when I'm about your age. We want to build it out in the country, and we've already started planning for it financially. Ask yourself seriously, is this still the dream? Talk about it as a family, and then use those financial resources in whatever way you think is the most valuable for you.

Most of all, never, ever stop dreaming. Your dreams of writing made The Simple Dollar possible and has (hopefully) led to some great writing opportunities over the last decade. Don't stop. Listen to what your heart is telling you and do it. You should be close to complete financial freedom now—-take that leap and just run with whatever it is that's in your heart.

Onc final thing: she still wants to go on that Bahamas trip, you know. See if you can leave the kids with her parents for a week or two and just go. It will probably be the best thing you guys have done since, well, your honeymoon.

Best wishes,

Your twenty nine year old self

No matter where my life goes between now and then, the contents of that letter will mean something when I read it again in 2018.

时间去体验一些新东西了。

现在，我们的家庭计划是在你那个年纪的时候建一所新房。我们想把房子建在郊区，并且已经开始计划筹钱了。认真地问问自己，这仍然是梦想吗？从一个家庭成员的角度来谈论这件事，然后把这些财务资源用在你认为最有价值的地方。

最重要的是，永远不要放弃梦想。你关于写作的梦想让《简单的美元》这本书成为可能，并有希望在过去 10 年给你带来一些很棒的写作机会。不要放弃。倾听你内心的声音，然后付诸实践。你现在应该接近财务自由——勇敢地去实现飞跃，然后带着内心的梦想奋力奔跑。

最后一件事：你知道，她仍然想去巴哈马群岛旅行。看看你能不能把孩子留给她父母带一两个星期，然后你们就出发。那将会是你们自蜜月以来度过的最美好的时光。

最美好的祝福，

29 岁的我

无论我的人生从现在起会经历什么，当我在 2018 年重读此信时，这封信的内容无疑对我意义重大。

Growth must be chosen again and again;

fear must be overcome again and again.

我们必须一次又一次选择成长，

一次又一次克服恐惧。